Reflections

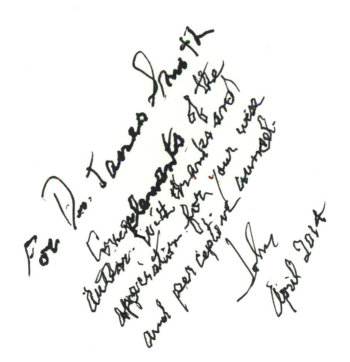

Books by John H. Rubel

Selected Poems
1940–1998

Memoirs I
Oft In The Stilly Night
1920–1942

Memoirs II
Air Of Other Summers
1942–1959

Memoirs III
Time And Chance
1959–1976

Doomsday Delayed: USAF Strategic Weapons Doctrine
and SIOP-62, 1959–1962, Two Cautionary Tales

Reflections

On Fame and Some Famous Men

John H. Rubel

SUNSTONE
PRESS

SANTA FE

Sunstone books may be purchased for educational, business, or sales promotional use.
For information please write: Special Markets Department, Sunstone Press,
P.O. Box 2321, Santa Fe, New Mexico 87504-2321.

Book design › Vicki Ahl
Body typeface › Minion Pro
Printed on acid free paper

Library of Congress Cataloging-in-Publication Data

Rubel, John H.
    Reflections on fame and some famous men / by John H. Rubel.
        p. cm.
    Includes bibliographical references.
    ISBN 978-0-86534-736-6 (softcover : alk. paper)
    1. Engineers--Biography. 2. Scientists--Biography. 3. Fame. I. Title.
TA139.R798 2009
909.82--dc22

                                    2009037662

WWW.SUNSTONEPRESS.COM
SUNSTONE PRESS / POST OFFICE BOX 2321 / SANTA FE, NM 87504-2321 /USA
(505) 988-4418 / ORDERS ONLY (800) 243-5644 / FAX (505) 988-1025

Ah, did you once see Shelley plain,
  And did he stop and speak to you?
And did you speak to him again?
  How strange it seems, and new!

But you were living before that,
  And also you are living after,
And the memory I started at—
  My starting moves your laughter!

I crossed a moor with a name of its own
  And a certain use in the world no doubt,
Yet a hand's breadth of it shines alone
  'Mid the blank miles round about—

For there I picked up on the heather
  And there I put inside my breast
A moulted feather, an eagle-feather—
  Well, I forget the rest.
                        —Robert Browning

What is fame,
but that men will know your name who never knew you,
and will never know themselves?
—Anon.

*TO
ROBIN*

My sweetheart

CONTENTS

ON REFLECTION ----------------------- 11

1 / EINSTEIN---------------------------- 16

2 / ROBERT A. MILLIKAN -------------- 20

3 / THEODORE VON KARMAN-------- 26

4 / WERNHER VON BRAUN----------- 33

5 / GENERAL CURTIS LE MAY --------- 56

6 / THE SKYBOLT CRISIS -------------- 72

7 / TENSING NORGAY ---------------- 101

8 / KURT MANKEN -------------------- 119

NOTES---------------------------------- 125

ON REFLECTION

By three methods we may learn wisdom:
first, by reflection, which is the noblest . . .
—Confucius

At starting I intended this book to consist of some short chapters about my encounters with a few famed or prominent people. Anecdotes about the famous, whether in biographies or the daily press, are there because they interest readers. I had not thought beyond imitating such examples. But the book quickly grew well beyond my first intentions. Indeed, the chief purpose of Chapter 1 about my brief encounter with Einstein is not about Einstein at all, but is instead a reflection on the fascinating emanations of fame, however transient these usually turn out to be. The famed, however—Galileo, Newton, Darwin and Einstein, for example—remain famous long after they die. Einstein is the only example in this volume. Just getting Einstein's autograph when I was ten years old, it seemed to me then, and still does, was *something*.

Einstein, as noted, is Chapter 1. Chapter 2 is Robert Millikan. As I grew up during the 1920s and

30s, his name was well known in educated circles as the second American physicist to earn the Nobel prize, awarded in 1923. During those decades he headed and transformed Caltech (the California Institute of Technology) from a minor school in a small Los Angeles suburb into a world-renowned scientific center. Millikan was a familiar presence on the Caltech campus during my four years there. I encountered him personally on several occasions. Still, recounting one of those encounters from nearly seventy years ago taught me more about Millikan than I had ever taken the trouble to learn before. His, I found, was not only a life to admire, but perhaps the closest of any in this volume to a life to envy as well.

Writing about Wernher von Braun, whom I knew only by reputation and from the few hours he was our dinner guest in Washington nearly fifty years ago, led to extended reading and long reflection on his trajectory from Hitler's *wunderkind* to a favorite of U.S. presidents and the U.S. Congress. To sum up the more detailed and puzzling account: I imagine the familiar statue of Justice, blindfolded, holding the scales of justice in her extended hand. What, in von Braun's case, appear on the scales?

On one side, his Nazi Party membership card; his commission as a colonel in the notorious Nazi SS; his leading involvement in decisions to transport concentration camp prisoners to underground factories producing the V-1 and V-2 German "vengeance" missiles, and his seeming indifference to the starvation, brutalizing, torture and ultimate extermination of almost all 27,000 slave laborers sent there.

On the other scale are piled his patriotic devotion to the German war effort; the exculpatory barbarous rule of Nazi Germany that co-opted him, not only, but especially during WWII; his pioneering leadership there and in the U.S. in rocket technology; the Redstone rockets developed by his team for the U.S. Army; his brilliant leadership of NASA's Saturn V Apollo rocket project that unerringly put men on the moon several times; the title of "professor" bestowed by Hitler; his writings and speeches about the essential truths of the Bible; and maybe his good looks and seductive charm.

These things do not have mass proportional to their moral weight. At some point, Justice must remove her blindfold and decide how these incommensurate constituents of the historical record are to be weighed. So must we, those of us who reflect upon our own moral universe, and that of others. Von Braun's story becomes not only a tale of his time and times; it displays the seemingly irresolvable moral conflict between ethically principled action on the one hand, and the often notable effectiveness of unprincipled expediency in the "real" world on the other.

The chapters about Gen. LeMay (Chapter 5) and the Skybolt Crisis (Chapter 6) are linked. In Chapter 5 we see the Skybolt missile project as a LeMay pet. If not its father, he was assuredly its midwife. Chapter 6 depicts the unfolding crisis that ensued.

Several once-well-known figures appear in Chapter 6, including Robert McNamara, his British counterparts Harold Watkinson and Peter Thorneycroft and the prolific British scientist Solly Zuckerman. President Eisenhower and Prime Minister Macmillan play a key role, Macmillan a long one. Gen. LeMay appeared at the beginning. President Kennedy appears at the end, wondering how the Skybolt Crisis happened (and swiftly commissioning a book-length study to find out).

The story is larger than any of its actors. It was so at the time. It remains a metaphor for how unintended consequences can and sometimes do erupt from acts and decisions taken in disparate layers of complex bureaucracies. It shows prominent, even some once-famous men on both sides of the Atlantic dealing at the highest level with a troubling high-stakes diplomatic crisis. Its history may yet be further elaborated as classified documents emerge to the light of day. I believe Chapter 6 is the latest summary contribution to that history, and the last written by one who witnessed the Skybolt episode almost from its larval origins to its final denouement.

To conclude: trying to write a little, I found myself reading a lot and reflecting at some depth about many of the people and events sketched here. I have been enlightened and enriched thereby. I hope the reader may be, too—and even, from time to time, entertained as well.

John Kenneth Galbraith, in the charming volume *Name Dropping,* writes that

> Reminiscence and anecdote, as they tell of one's meetings with the great or the prominent, are an established form of self-enhancement. They make known that one was there. . . The risk . . . exists that critics may suggest that I am indulging in name-dropping. . . [But] nothing so disarms a prosecutor as a prior confession of guilt.

I could not have said it better. I make the same disclaimer: name-dropping, even if confessed, was not my object.

I am deeply indebted to Ron Landa, of the Historical Office of the Secretary of Defense, for his invaluable assistance in the composition of Chapter 6. His own writings on the subject rekindled my interest in the Skybolt Crisis many decades after the events recounted there. He furnished me with declassified documents, many of British origin, to which I would otherwise have had no access. He read several drafts of the chapter with great attention to accuracy and detail. At his suggestion, Chapter 6 includes endnotes identifying sources to enhance its utility among students of the Skybolt episode.

I am likewise grateful to Graeme Kelleher, who supplied transcripts of Tenzing Norgay's (Chapter 7) talks on our Nepal trek, additional anecdotes and many helpful comments and emendations.

I thank my wife, Robin, who read several drafts of the book and discovered numerous errors, as she usually does. Those that remain are mine alone.

1

EINSTEIN

The first famous person I ever saw up close was Albert Einstein. It was in early spring, 1931. I was almost eleven. I had read or heard that Einstein was visiting Caltech in nearby Pasadena (we lived in Los Angeles). I asked my grandmother if she would take me to Caltech (we had no car in those days. She had a driver). I wanted to get Einstein's autograph. I learned that Einstein was probably lunching at the stately Atheneum, only recently completed, which served then and now as a faculty club and residence for distinguished visitors.

I waited on the brick walk just below the low steps leading up to the Atheneum's atrium entrance. Shortly after 1 PM Einstein emerged, accompanied by Robert Millikan, who fathered and led Caltech, and several others whose somewhat rumpled look matched my expectations. The group descended the last shallow stone steps where I stood on the brick walk. I approached them as they approached me. Extending my leather-bound autograph book in his direction, I asked Einstein for his autograph. He signed the book.

Nearly seventy years after my first and only encounter with Einstein, my wife Robin's sister wondered if I could arrange to have her son and his Japanese fiancée married at the Atheneum. I had been a member of the Atheneum for a long time. I made the necessary arrangements. The young couple came over from Japan, along with numerous Japanese family members who, except for the Japanese bride, spoke no English. The wedding took place on the atrium entranceway, at the top of the broad, shallow stairs at the bottom of which I had obtained Einstein's autograph. It was another perfect Pasadena spring day.

The wedding party gathered after the ceremony for dinner in the small Atheneum library. I gave a short talk for the benefit of the Japanese visitors, outlining the building's history. It had been built in the years following the Crash of 1929 for something like $500,000, a faculty club and domicile for visiting dignitaries, of which Einstein was the first. I described how the faculty had been gathering for lunch in the dining room just steps away ever since it opened in 1931, discussing such epoch-making things as Hubble's discovery of the expanding universe, Morgan's identification of the gene, Anderson's discovery of the positron, Pauling's pioneering work on the chemical bond, Zwicky's many newly identified supernovae, and how, when not quite eleven, I had stood at the bottom of the same steps where we had all stood only minutes before, and secured Einstein's signature. The bridegroom and bride translated as I spoke each sentence.

The Japanese were visibly interested. One young lady asked if I thought that Einstein might have sat on the very chair on which she was then sitting. There were only a few chairs in the small library, apart from the dining chairs brought in for the occasion. I replied that yes, he very well might have. A momentary silence fell. She gazed for a moment into a remote distance. Mark, the bridegroom, told me later that all this had impressed his Japanese in-laws and improved his prestige in their eyes.

Herb York once pointed out to me that since he had met, say, President Eisenhower, as he had before I did, then I, who knew Herb, was "once-met" with Eisenhower. So the party ended on a memorable note, with a dozen or so Japanese happily once-met with Einstein.

2

ROBERT A MILLIKAN

Einstein was world-famed, but Robert A. Millikan was by far the most famous *American* scientist during the 1920s and 30s. Although he bore the modest title of Chairman of the Executive Council at Caltech, few had any idea of who else was on the Council, and everybody, including its members, knew perfectly well that Millikan ran Caltech. This is not the place to recount, but only to remind the reader that Millikan was a Nobel Laureate in physics. He was best known among undergraduates for having devised a delicate experiment by means of which he accurately determined the value of the electrical charge on the electron. Further, he showed that all electrons have the same charge. Less known were his studies that definitively confirmed atomic theories of matter, including his experimental verification of Einstein's photoelectric equation. He continued studying cosmic rays for many years, even while authoring many books and leading Caltech to global stardom as a world center of contemporary science in many disciplines.

On December 7, 1941, in my senior Caltech year, the Japanese bombed Pearl Harbor. A few days later, Hitler declared war on the United States. The attack quickly mobilized public outrage and aligned public sentiment, much of it strongly pacifist until then, in a readiness to fight. It also aroused dread of sabotage or attack, both of which were widely feared in a multitude of imagined forms, especially on the West Coast. Dr. Millikan quickly appointed a committee charged with taking measures to increase the security of the Caltech campus and prepare for possible enemy attacks, presumably from Japan.

Within days it became clear that there were many dimensions to the business of protecting the campus. The Committee set up by Millikan asked for student help. I was appointed the student representative to the Committee, charged with organizing whatever student participation it decided to require.

The Committee met in a small classroom room somewhere on the second floor of Throop Hall, the oldest classroom building on campus, which also housed the administrative offices. The meeting room was empty except for a library table and a few armless chairs. The Committee's first chairman was Prof. Michael, a civil engineer, well known on campus for his popular yearly lecture on the scientific aspects of trout fishing.

The Committee included professors of physics, chemistry, biology, geology and history. It called for courses to be given by faculty experts in poison gas detection and decontamination. I and a couple of hundred students volunteered to attend what turned out to be popular and grimly fascinating lectures and demonstrations that greatly enhanced our ability to imagine the catastrophic and seemingly unstoppable consequences of a poison gas attack.

Franz Zwicky, famed for his many discoveries of supernovae

and his claim to have skied over the top of the Mt. Wilson telescope dome in winter, conducted extended experiments on the effect of pasting cellophane on windows. The idea was to protect people against flying glass shattered by bomb explosions. The British, he said, had discovered the utility of "zellophane" pasted on windows with "treacle." Everyone, including Zwicky, had heard of treacle, in Dickens if nowhere else, but nobody knew what it was. The dictionary says it is a kind of syrup. Somewhere it was intimated that treacle was sugar water.

We pasted a lot of cellophane on dorm windows to test the durability of treacle and other glues we compounded or bought. All of them worked fine for a while. All, we soon discovered, failed after a few weeks of exposure to the Pasadena sun, leaving a miscellany of multicolored cellophane strips dangling from dorm windows for untold months.

Meanwhile, Committee members presented strong cases for conflicting tactics. Geology was firm: first, the Japanese would ignite the foothills with incendiary bombs. Refugees would flood the campus, loaded with flammable possessions. Allowed to congregate there, they would be burned alive as foothill fires spread to the valley below. That, we were assured, was precisely what had happened in the Japanese earthquake of 1923. So the students' job was to keep people moving. Don't let them congregate on the open spaces of the campus, surrounded by flammable possessions.

Chemistry disagreed. The Japanese would shatter all the campus windows with high-explosive bombs. Terrified refugees would flock to the Caltech basements. The water lines feeding the campus would be bombed. The hapless refugees below ground would be trapped and drowned as water flooded the basements in which they would be taking shelter. So the students had to ensure that the water mains would be shut off upon warning of an impending attack. Chemistry did not object to turning the water off, but insisted that, drowning aside, the poison gases the Japanese would drop, being heavier than air, would seep through the bombed-out basement windows, with results too horrible to recount if refugees were allowed to congregate there.

Despite such disagreements, or perhaps because of them, many measures were implemented through a comprehensive organization of student volunteers which I headed. We were ready to shelter refugees or shoo them off the campus, whatever was decided. We had squads alerted seven-twenty-four to turn off the water mains. We inventoried all the gas masks in Pasadena (there appeared to be only one, somewhere in the Fire Department.) All this took a lot of time and the efforts of dozens of students.

One of the Committee's jobs was to figure out how to protect the "Old Dorm." It was the rickety, decaying, two-story "temporary" building built for cadets during WWI, more than twenty years before, now housing the Greasy Spoon café and a few graduate students in a primitive upstairs dormitory. There was not and could not be any adequate fire protection in or around the Old Dorm. It was an obvious fire hazard.

The Old Dorm problem was discussed at length in several committee meetings, but, in the absence of any nearby fire hydrants, the only idea that got much traction was a bucket-brigade of students furnished with a large pile of sand that might be set up near the building. That idea presented the daunting problem of getting buckets of sand from the ground up to the top of a two-story blazing inferno with nothing at hand but men on the ground holding the buckets. Since the problem had no practical solution, and nobody could think of anything better, nothing was done.

One day, after a couple of months of meetings and a great many activities, but without progress on the Old Dorm, Prof. Michael announced at the start of a meeting that Dr. Millikan was going to attend for the first time in the Committee's brief existence. A somber silence descended. Nobody spoke. Nobody moved. A pensive air settled over the room. As we sat there, each wrapped in his own thoughts, I reflected on the men around the table, all of them well launched on distinguished academic careers, most old enough to be my father and young enough to be Millikan's son, nervously musing on his arrival, and on my impressions of Dr. Millikan himself.

He was then 74 years old, but he neither looked nor acted like the image I had then of a man that age. He was of medium height and build and, as I see him now in my mind's eye, trim and erect with an athletic bearing and an energetic air about him, radiating vigor and self-assured authority. His was by no means merely the charisma of the powerful executive, the Chairman of Caltech's Executive Council. He was, after all, America's most famous living scientist. He was an *American* Nobel Laureate whose family had lived in America for some two hundred years. He remained, after many decades, a brilliant experimental physicist who also knew how to operate in the world of non-scientific affairs. He commanded respect wherever he went, not least among faculty members a generation younger. What, I wondered, would these now-somber faculty leaders, eminent men, committee-men, do when Millikan arrived?

The door burst open. Millikan strode in looking neither right nor left. To a man we leapt to our feet with a single motion. In a flash the eminent professors crowded and shoved as each offered a chair to Millikan. He ignored them all as he strode to the head of the table, where he sat down in Prof. Michael's seat and without preliminaries, began to speak.

"I am very displeased with the work of this committee," he said. His chief concern was the danger of fire in the Old Dorm. "What has been done about that?," he demanded. Prof. Michael started to highlight the seemingly insurmountable difficulties. He mentioned the sand pile. Millikan interrupted with a gesture of impatience. "It's all very simple," he declared. "There is even a book about Civil

Defense. You can buy it in any bookstore. They sell it in all the drugstores. It tells all about what to do in case of attack. All you have to do is fill the bathtub with water and have a bucket handy."

Everybody except, evidently, Dr. Millikan, knew that there were no bathtubs in the Old Dorm, or that if there were they would be useless in the face of a major fire. The building was a tinder box. He probably knew it, too, but nobody dared challenge him. Nobody said a word. He soon got to the point: Prof. Michael was replaced as chairman by Prof. J. Wallace Sterling, not a scientist, not even an engineer, but a professor of history, later to become president of Stanford University, whereupon Millikan left as unceremoniously as he had entered.

With that change we carried on as before to the end of the quarter. Wartime replaced peacetime across the land. Final exams came quickly, then graduation. School and the Committee closed for the summer. I and the seniors who had manned the campus defense teams left for life in the real world. Bemused by the ambiguities of brilliance and power so briefly but indelibly displayed by Millikan and the professors had given me a valuable early glimpse into how some things work out there.

Millikan ruled Caltech for several more years. So far as I know, the Old Dorm problem was never solved. After the war, they tore it down.

3

THEODORE VON KARMAN

In early November 1940, just about everyone at Caltech, where I was a junior, and every aeronautical scientist and engineer in universities and industry, knew that Theodore von Kármán was the leader of American aeronautical science. He had been the head of Caltech's graduate school of aeronautics and director of the Guggenheim Aeronautical Laboratory at the California Institute of Technology (GALCIT) for a decade. Galcit was the proud possessor of the largest wind-tunnel west of the Mississippi. It was much used by Douglas Aircraft, Northrop, North American, Lockheed and other major airplane design and manufacturing companies in the Los Angeles basin. But until a few days after the collapse of the Tacoma Narrows Bridge in a stiff but comparatively modest wind storm on November 7 (exactly sixty years ago as I write), I had never been in von Kármán's presence.

The collapse of the Tacoma Narrows bridge was a seminal event in the annals of bridge design. No such bridge had ever been known to fail owing to "flutter," an unfamiliar concept except for a few specialists, in those days. For one thing, the catastrophe had been extensively photographed as the bridge began to sway and undulate in comparatively modest winds as the storm started, and then, as the wind picked up, very rapidly collapsed almost explosively with a swift series of sinuous, self-destroying motions that nobody had ever seen or imagined possible for a once-magnificent suspension bridge made of steel and concrete.

Newspapers carried vivid pictures and newsreels played motion pictures showing parts of the bridge roadway, more than a mile long, distorted by huge twists and snake-like vertical undulations moments before huge chunks flew from it and a whole section of roadway collapsed into the waters below. Nothing like this had ever been caught on film before. For us, last year's sophomores, it was a mystery. Bridge designers were well informed about early iron bridges that collapsed from fatigue failures induced by resonant vibrations that were briefly but fatally amplified by the rhythmical marching of army troops. But this was different.

Although they knew about it in Tacoma, we had not heard that the Tacoma Narrows bridge was so unusually flexible that, in the few months it had been in use since opening to traffic in early July 1940, it had earned the nickname *Galloping Gertie* from the undulations of its roadway in even modest winds. Of course, as children, almost everyone quickly learns how to make big waves slosh in the bathtub by moving back and forth at just the right rhythm. Likewise, winds recurring in rhythmical gusts could, conceivably, have excited similar resonant vibrations causing this catastrophe (resonance is still, incorrectly, cited as the cause in some textbooks), but the winds that destroyed the Tacoma bridge were not rhythmical.

Rather, apart from occasional random gusts, the wind blew fairly steadily, but as the storm progressed, their velocity rose from modest speeds to somewhat over forty miles per hour. The question remains: how could largely steady winds set up the destructive motions that tore the vast steel and concrete structure apart in seconds?

We were discussing all this when, for the first and last time ever during my Caltech years, von Kármán walked in. He picked up on the conversation right away. "It is very simple," he declared. "It was flutter." He said this in an accent that can only be characterized as Kármán, a mixture of Hungarian, German and perhaps other languages. In any case, none of us knew what "flutter" meant.

As I learned later, flutter can occur when a body, such as an airplane wing or, in this case, a suspension bridge, having certain elastic properties, is deflected from its rest position by a more or less steady wind. Suppose, as happened in the Tacoma Narrows bridge case, the wind is strong enough to make the bridge sway from side-to-side. That motion requires at least part of the roadway to twist, since the ends are anchored. Twisting causes the force exerted on the long roadway by the wind to increase, much as you noticed when, as a child, you loved to hold your hand into the wind outside the window of a moving car, twisting it just a little to feel the sharp increase in the lifting force that, unresisted, would raise your hand and twist it even further.

A giant suspension bridge, paved in concrete laid over a steel framework firmly attached to enormous foundations at both ends, does resist twisting. Elastic forces in the steelwork momentarily deformed by the wind make it twist back. At some point, the elastic restoring forces exceed the wind's lifting force, and the bridge snaps back. Since it has gained momentum by absorbing wind energy, it snaps to a more severe twist in the counter direction. The wind forces pressing on this amplified twist are thereby strengthened. As the elastic forces again overcome wind forces, the bridge snaps back with added momentum and twists even further than the time before. Assuming the wind continues blow, as it does past a moving airplane, and as it did during the Tacoma storm, only a few such cycles are enough to overstress parts. When a few cables break from the twisting stresses, as they did, the remaining cables, and other structural members depending from them, are and were stressed even more. Swiftly, a cascade of failures led to catastrophe.

As for "flutter:" since the bridge will not only twist in the wind, but undulate, as wind and mechanical forces combine to lift portions of the span, much of the huge roadway and its supporting cables will appear to flutter, not unlike the complex rippling of a flag. Von Kármán, who knew about flutter from his work with aircraft, realized at what was then the first time, that flutter had caused a major suspension bridge to self-destruct.

Soon after, he was appointed to the board of inquiry investigating collapse. He discovered that an agent for the Merchant's Fire Assurance Company, subsequently charged with grand larceny, had pocketed the premiums paid by the State of Washington for $800,000 worth of insurance that was never paid for. The agent appears to have had the confidence shared by uncounted millions in the seeming solidity of a bridge made of steel and concrete, serenely majestic in calm weather.

One year later, December 1941, the U.S. entered WWII. Von Kármán, already sixty years old, took an active role in the development of solid propellant rockets and rocket fuel for military uses. In 1944, the war still raging in both Europe and the Pacific, three years before the Air Force became independent from the Army, its chief, General "Hap" Arnold, asked him to spearhead a study identifying the scientific and technological research and development projects the Air Force should support for the next 10-20-30 years. In 1945, again at Gen. Arnold's request, Kármán headed a committee charged with finding out everything it could about German aeronautical developments during WWII. Two years later, the newly independent United States Air Force created the Air Force Science Advisory Committee, chaired by von Kármán. Many USAF technological initiatives were introduced under his leadership and sustained by his prestige.

I did not see Kármán again until twenty years after that first encounter in 1940. By then, I was an official in the Pentagon. He was Science Advisor to the commander of NATO. It happened one day in early 1960 that I bumped into two colleagues, on a Paris boulevard, whom I had known for years. One, Marvin Vavra, worked at the Hughes Aircraft Co. where I had worked before going to Washington. The other, Ernie Roberts, was a rocket engineer at Aerojet General, a company in which Kármán was an early investor. Roberts had emigrated from Hungary. Vavra, too, was of Hungarian origin. Both knew Kármán. They invited to me to accompany them for a visit to his apartment.

Barbara Talbot, his student more than thirty years before when he taught at the university at Aachen, answered the door. She was a beautiful woman, approaching sixty. Like many in what once had been Alsace-Lorraine, she was a German national with a French name. We assumed she was a widow. Her husband, Talbot, a former Wehrmacht officer, had been a scion of a wealthy German family known, in better days, as the leading if not the sole supplier of railway sleeping cars in Germany. Before the war she had lived as the chatelaine of a large estate. During the war, German Army officers commandeered much of her home. Americans replaced the Germans as Allied forces advanced into Germany. The Americans, she said, were vandals, who had left her fine home severely damaged.

Kármán was now about eighty, but as witty and almost as energetic as I remembered him twenty years before. Kármán and Barbara Talbot had recently returned from visiting Israel, then a new nation only a dozen years from its war for independence in 1948. Kármán asked us if we knew what the Israelis called the

German Jews among them. We did not. "Dzey say," he pronounced in his inimitable accent, "dzhat dzey combine Chewish modesty vit Prussian charm!" A stream of comparable witticisms followed.

Von Kármán was born in Hungary in 1881. He was the oldest representative of the extraordinary group of Hungarian Jewish scientists, von Neumann, Teller, Wigner and Szilard among them, that came of age in the first quarter of the last century, rising to eminence soon enough to escape the European Holocaust. In 1930, growing political unrest and rising anti-Semitism in Aachen led Kármán to accept Caltech's offer to become director of what became the renowned Aeronautical Laboratory there. In his later years, as this Hungarian refugee coterie rose to world renown in scientific circles, von Kármán would volunteer in public addresses that he had been asked where he and his fellow Hungarians had really come from. "We are Martians," he would say, his way of subtly acknowledging that they were, indeed, outsiders, forever strangers in a strange land, but endowed with spectacularly superior, and for them, life-saving intellectual powers,.

Some months later, still a Pentagon official, I was asked to give a talk at a large meeting called by General Arthur Trudeau, then serving as the Army's military head of research and development. Other speakers were drawn from universities, the aerospace industry and government offices. The large audience included many others from these venues. Von Kármán was there. The speakers were supposed to cover various aspects of military aircraft and missile development.

A couple of hours into the conference a news story broke, reporting that a scheduled test launch of an Atlas intercontinental ballistic missile at Cape Canaveral had been canceled because a sandwich had been discovered in a liquid oxygen ("LOX") line. This, as the Cold War missile race gathered momentum, was headline news. General Trudeau, who thrived on press coverage, had been called away mid-morning by newsmen eager for quotable comments. Did he think this could have been sabotage? Well, yes, *certainly* it could have been. That made more headlines, accompanied by inanities: had it been a *lox* sandwich in the LOX line?

This interruption over, I delivered my short talk. I had researched the mounting cost of producing airframes in the U.S. I presented a chart showing that for several decades the cost of airframe per pound had been mounting exponentially, meaning at a nearly fixed annual rate of growth. "Airframe" means the plane's body, wings, tail and landing gear alone, without engines, propellers (if any), or any equipment or furnishings inside.

Projecting my chart into the future showed that in another few decades the entire 1960 defense budget would be required to pay for just two B-52 airframes. I mentioned, in passing, that the proposed B-70 bomber airframe, though not yet in production, already cost more than its weight in gold. The data were indisputable. Conclusions varied. My observations were not received with much enthusiasm among military customers and their industrial suppliers. Subsequent speakers commented that while gold had no intrinsic value, the same surely could not be said of the B-70 bomber.

I had been seated next to von Kármán in the front row of the auditorium. I sat there again after my talk. Kármán wore a hearing aid. It consisted of a large earpiece connected by an electric cord to a small box at his waist. There was a volume control on the box. Kármán leaned over toward me as he readjusted the volume control. "Zhat," he said, *soto voce* near my ear, "vas dze best piece uff fizdom vhat ve haff had all day!"

I have flattered myself ever since that he wasn't kidding.

4

WERNHER VON BRAUN

The Space Age opened to the public when the Soviet satellite, Sputnik 1, began circling the globe on October 4, 1957. Until then, few Americans had ever thought about an artificial satellite, or were even quite clear about just what such a thing would be. But there it was, a shining object moving visibly among the stars and, if you had a radio handy, sending out a *beep-beep-beep* full of some meaning, a greeting or a warning, or both. It meant space technology, some kind of huge rocket, a Soviet "first," something in the sky, a bright, star-like object moving among the stars, a symbol of military power, a portent of danger.

VON BRAUN

America's first attempt to launch a satellite a few weeks later, powered by a Navy Vanguard sounding rocket, blew up almost immediately after launching. In part because Eisenhower wanted to avoid casting a military taint on America's contribution to the International Geophysical Year, he had vetoed using an Air Force or Army missile-related rocket as a launch vehicle for the Explorer 1 satellite, but, reluctantly, after the globally broadcast failure of the first attempt, he finally agreed to allow a Juno-1 modified Redstone, a descendant of the infamous German V-2, a von Braun rocket developed at the Army's Redstone Arsenal, to be used. The next launch attempt was near the end of January 1958, only weeks after the previous failure. Both the launch and the mission were splendidly successful. Two weeks later, von Braun's picture appeared on the cover of TIME magazine. The first successful American space shot had been made so by Wernher von Braun.

He had been the rocket *wunderkind* in Hitler's Germany. Now he had become America's. He was photographed with presidents. Congress fell for him. In the American popular mind the super-scientist—Einstein, Szilard, von Neumann, Lisa Meitner—was vaguely foreign and more or less German. So was von Braun—German, a Doctor, author of the V-2 and handsomely charming to boot. He became the archetype of the "rocket scientist," a species conjured in the American imagination.

I never worked with von Braun. During most of my Washington years in the Defense Department von Braun worked for NASA, the non-military space agency, transferred there from the Army in mid-1960, where his rocket work no longer served demonstrable military purposes. I did, however, work with the top levels of NASA management throughout my years in the Pentagon where figures like Hugh Dryden, James Webb, and especially, Bob Seamans, as well as many others, carried vast responsibilities for the skillful management of the greatest space ventures ever undertaken. Still, to this day, Wernher von Braun's name is most likely the only one, apart from an astronaut or two, remembered by that fraction of the public that can recall the birth of the Space Age. Even as his fame grew, however, it was not uncommon to hear von Braun's fame derided in many circles as the former Hitler hero, Nazi Party member, Wehrmacht and SS officer and consummate opportunist, whose picture now appeared on the Wheaties box in every American grocery store and millions of breakfast tables. I was among the cynics. First: some background.

FAMILY ROOTS

Briefly: von Braun came into the world in 1912 with an enviable pedigree and perfect timing for one destined to become infatuated with the charms of space travel. Von Braun's father descended from a long line of Prussian Junker nobility. He spoke three languages fluently. He entered the German civil service as a young man and managed to land on his feet again and again during the tempestuous years of WWI, the post-war rise of the Weimar Republic, and the rise and fall of Hitler's Third Reich. Never overly fond of democracy, he turned to banking, and emerged from the disastrous hyper-inflation of the early 1920s still prosperous and able to send Wernher and his other children to exclusive private schools. Von Braun's mother was descended from European medieval royalty on both her father's and her mother's side and, like her husband, belonged to the upper strata of Prussian Junker nobility, in her case one with a strong intellectual and cultural tradition. She spoke six languages.

Fascinated by space travel and rocketry in his teens, von Braun managed to serve as an assistant to Hermann Oberth, the German rocket pioneer, in early experiments with liquid fuel rocket motors, when he was only 18 years old. Brilliant from childhood, he was soon inspired to plunge into serious study, and handily earned his PhD degree in physics at 22.

HITLER, ROCKETS, VON BRAUN

German civilian rocket societies were forbidden by the new Nazi regime in 1933. Von Braun joined the German Army's Ordnance Department upon finishing his schooling in 1934. Rocket activities were moved to Peenemünde on the North Sea three years later, a site suggested by his mother, whose family estates were in the vicinity. There he joined the Nazi Party. Three years after that he became an SS officer.

German forces invaded Poland in 1939. In 1940 they moved against France. By then, von Braun had been working on liquid-fueled rockets for much of the preceding decade. Hitler and his Reich were ascendant beyond all expectation. Already, in the spring of 1939, Army colonel (later Major-General) Dr. Walter Dornberger, von Braun's superior, was pressing forward with plans to begin production of the A-4 rocket, precursor of the V-2.

Neither von Braun nor his long-time associate both in Germany and the U.S., Arthur Rudolph, had any expertise in large-scale production. Hoping to secure backing he was not getting from the Army, Dornberger arranged for Hitler to visit a launch site in the spring of 1939. Von Braun, twenty-seven years old, briefed Hitler, but Hitler had other things on his mind, among them, consolidating his recent conquest of Czechoslovakia and planning the invasion of Poland. He seemed to take little interest in prospects for this speculative rocket venture. Emphasis shifted to here-and-now military demands. Priorities granted earlier to the V-2 project were threatened.

Then, in the spring of 1940, an SS colonel visited von Braun, saying that Reichsfuehrer SS Himmler, the notorious chief of the SS, urged him to join. According to von Braun's account, he hesitated. Dornberger told him the SS had long been trying to get its "finger in the pie" at Peenemünde, and "that . . . if [he] wanted to continue our mutual work, [he] had no alternative but to join [the SS]." Von Braun was swept ever closer to the barbaric vortex at the heart of the Nazi regime as the SS began to push the Army out of its way at Peenemünde.

By early 1941 the army at last got Peenemünde's development priority restored, but not the same high priority for the production plant. On June 22 Germany's gigantic assault on the Soviet Union began. Hitler, vastly overconfident of victory, shifted priorities to the Luftwaffe and the Navy in preparation for a renewed military effort against the U.K. The Army chief, von Brauchitsch, arranged for Hitler to sit for another briefing on the V-2. Dornberger, von Braun and others met with the Fuhrer in his high-security east-Prussian "Wolf's Lair" outpost on August 20.

This time Hitler's reaction was over the top. He saw the V-2 as a revolutionary future weapon. If successfully developed, he declared, hundreds of thousands a year must be produced. Now von Braun became immersed in efforts to prepare for production of a missile that had not yet been successfully flight-tested, two years after Dornberger had begun pushing for just that. Hitler, however, awaited a successful flight test before supporting production.

The first completely successful flight test of the A-4 was achieved at last, more than a year later, following a long series of failures. This was the world's first, a ballistic missile that reached the edge of space 56 miles above the earth, and landed in the Baltic 118 miles away. It was October 3, 1942. Now von Braun would be forced to concentrate far more on production, pressured from the top, still facing development problems constantly bubbling up from below.

WANSEE, DOOMED PRISONERS, PRODUCTION

But by July 1943, circumstances had greatly changed. Germany had declared war against the U.S. eighteen months before. Within weeks, the Final Solution of the "Jewish Problem" had been quickly settled in January 1942 at a short, notorious meeting among representatives of various German governmental and military departments at the Berlin suburb, Wansee. Now millions of Jews were being systematically rounded up and transported to rapidly constructed death camps. Those who appeared at a short glance to the selection official—usually a medical doctor—to be too old, or too young, or too feeble to work were sent immediately to the gas chambers. The others were spared to be worked to death. When they died from starvation, overwork, disease, maltreatment or execution they would be replaced by others, thus providing a virtually unlimited supply of workers for war production.

At the same time, the Russian campaign was not going well. A miracle weapon became ever-more appealing to Nazi leaders. A stream of high-level visitors—Minister of War Production and Armaments Albert Speer; Grand Admiral Karl Donitz; Luftwaffe Field Marshall Erhard Milch; and many others—had been pouring through Peenemünde as interest in the ballistic missile grew. Now Speer arranged for yet another briefing for Hitler at his eastern redoubt around July 7, 1943.

The Fuhrer appeared, accompanied by Speer and some top generals. A great black cape covered his bent shoulders. He looked tired and pale. The October 3 film of the first successful A-4 launch was shown, narrated by von Braun. It ended. Silence fell. Hitler had ordered the last, futile offensive on the Eastern Front only two days earlier, and was in a good mood. The silence was broken as he waxed almost fanatically enthusiastic. Dornberger, who had been pushing the A-4 development as a potentially war-winning breakthrough, now cautioned Hitler not to believe it was a "wonder weapon." It could not carry a larger warhead. It could not be produced in quantity for years.

To no avail. Hitler's eyes lit up with a fanatical light. "But what I want is annihilation—annihilating effect!" he proclaimed. Henceforth, Hitler took "great interest in the production planning for the A-4 [V-2]." He believed that, were it produced in adequate numbers, it would greatly impress the British. He spoke of hundreds of thousands of missiles, launched simultaneously in great numbers. As the Peenemünde group was leaving, Hitler took von Braun's hand and addressed him as "Professor," thus bestowing upon him a prestigious title that was normally accorded to university academics as a high government honor. Von Braun's German team continued to address him as "Professsor" even after coming to the U.S., until he dropped it rather than go into its dubious origin.

In early April, Arthur Rudolf, one of von Braun's chief assistants and a long-time friend, returned from a visit to a huge Heinkel Aircraft factory near Berlin, operated with prison labor. He was enthusiastic—the SS takes care of everything: clothing, food, housing, guarding. The factory just has to manage. Secrecy is better protected using prisoners than foreign workers. Prisoners that wear out are easily replaced. The Peenemünde administration under Dornberger, von Braun and Rudolph, but increasingly subject to SS direction and influence, proceeded to recruit hundreds of prisoners from the notorious Buchenwald concentration camp and house them in the Peenemünde complex.

In America, after the war, Von Braun said as little as possible about his role in using or his contacts with prisoner labor. Speaking to the science fiction writer, Arthur Clarke around the late 1960s or early 1970s, he said he never knew what was happening in the concentration camps, but suspected it, and despises himself for having failed to find out, which he could easily have done. He appears to have been referring to Jewish Holocaust victims, not to the prisoners working on the V-2, though many of these *were* Jews, all of whom were intended for ultimate extermination. All the prisoners were abused, tortured, barbarically overworked, starved, and all but a relative handful among thousands died or was wantonly murdered in the end. Speer, during the 1960s, denied knowledge of Nazi genocide, which was not only unbelievable, but was proved to be false. It would appear that von Braun's statements took much of their color and content from Speer's earlier ones, often claiming that he had never seen prisoners abused in the V-2 production works. Both of them—Speer from his widely read writings both during and after his long imprisonment in Spandau, and von Braun from his rare statements and meteoric American career—managed to create a remarkably laundered public self-image, each in his own way.

PROMOTIONS, ATTACKS, NORDHAUSEN TUNNELS

In late June 1943, production at Peenemünde proceeding at last, Himmler promoted von Braun to the rank of SS major. Hitler had already made Dornberger a brigadier general. Then, in mid-August, after a pleasant party that broke up about 11 PM, sirens shrieked, aircraft could be heard approaching, followed soon after by a massive bombing attack with some 600 British bombers that dropped nearly 2,000 tons of bombs. Several hundred prisoners and more than a hundred German staff were killed. Buildings were set on fire, essential secret documents were endangered and facilities suffered extensive damage.

A week later, on August 25, 1943, von Braun chaired a meeting discussing moving production to some caves in western Germany. He then flew to Berlin, where it was decided that production would be moved to the underground tunnels of an abandoned gypsum mine, located near Nordhausen in the Harz Mountains of north-central Germany. Three days later, the first group of Buchenwald prisoners was trucked to the tunnels to complete their excavation and prepare them for V-2 production. The facility was placed under SS control. SS General Hans Kammler, who, among his signal accomplishments, had designed the gas chambers and crematoria for many death camps, built Auschwitz-Birkenau, Mauthausen and others, and taken charge of the demolition of the Warsaw ghetto, built and supervised this one, employing the corporate skills of Mittelwerk GmBH, set up to handle challenging management details. It was built expressly as a death camp. Prisoners were to be used up until they died or, when no longer useful, killed. In the ethical language of Nazi Germany, these were "lives unworthy of life." What suffering they endured did not matter—they were certain to die soon anyway.

Within a few months a ladder-work of forty-six lateral tunnels, each about six-hundred feet long, connecting two curving parallel tunnels each more than a mile long, was largely completed, making a total of about a million square feet of underground floor space surmounted by ceilings more than three-stories high, wide enough for railroad trains to pass. At first there were no facilities to house the prisoners. Some 10,000 were jammed in the tunnels they were digging under inhuman conditions, worked to exhaustion in twelve-hour shifts, with no sanitary facilities, confined to the tunnels for weeks at a time, sick and dying from dysentery, typhus and other diseases. The dead were trucked back to Buchenwald to be cremated. Some of the half-dead, no longer worth feeding, were transported to Auschwitz and other death camps to be gassed. Eventually, a ramshackle camp, Dora, was set up to house prisoners outside the tunnels.

THE DORA COMPLEX; MASS MURDER

Before the war ended, Dora included a network of twenty-three branch camps and related facilities, most in a restricted military area surrounding Nordhausen. Some 20,000 workers—some say 27,000—died from starvation, exposure, overwork and torture, three times as many as were killed by the 3,000 missiles launched against putatively military targets, including London. Five-thousand died enlarging the tunnel system in the first three months alone. Many, suspected of sabotage, died under interrogation. Several hundred were publicly hanged for sabotage, real or suspected, where they died by slow strangulation and were left hanging for a few days in the tunnels and later in a public gallows set up in the Dora camp nearby. When the Germans retreated before advancing Allied forces in March-April 1945, thousands were shot on forced marches. Many, too weak to walk, were left to die on the roads. Several thousand were locked in a large barn and burned to death when the Germans set it on fire. Witnesses have reported that von Braun and many of his team from Peenemünde repeatedly walked through the V-2 factory at Mittelwerk and at satellite facilities, where he witnessed the condition of the workers and passed right next to heaps of dead prisoners who, unable to work, had been tortured to death by their SS guards. Some 6,700 unburied corpses were discovered when U.S. forces overran Dora soon after von Braun and his team had taken the train for the Bavarian Alps. In his Peenemünde days he had presided over at least one meeting of which records survive in which the allocation of concentration camp labor was on the agenda. One can only speculate that one recorded episode scarcely accounts for at least some, if not a number of unrecorded discussions and decisions involving prisoner labor. He was known to have been personally involved in selecting more than a thousand inmates with technical skills from Buchenwald to be transported to Mittelwerk.

Von Braun did his best to dodge questions about such matters during his decades in the U.S. He lied about them when interviewed by the Army before coming, saying he was unaware of prisoner mistreatment, which eye-witness accounts directly contradict. Neither von Braun nor any of his relatives, ever submitted to questions touching on Mittlewerk-Dora or von Braun's moral amnesia, not to mention complicities, as a leading figure linked to the

Nazi underworld of horrors. His intimate involvement was slow to become public even after passage of the Freedom of Information Act in 1966, although the essence of most of it could be readily inferred from the publicly known barbarities of the Nazi regime. Many, my mother included, did. Many did not care. Many still don't. Whatever the U.S. Army had on record regarding all this remained classified and unexamined for years after von Braun and his team came to the U.S. in 1945. Much did not surface until undisclosed documents and writings by survivors appeared decades later, much of it after he died in 1977.

V-1 and V-2

Von Braun had been briefly imprisoned after making some pessimistic remarks at a party, an episode that he often recounted when interviewed in the U.S. by way of establishing his anti-Nazi *bona fides*. On the other hand, anybody who knew there was a war going on had read and heard about the V-1 cruise missiles and V-2 ballistic missiles fired from Germany and northern France, exploding with fearsome consequences in London. The V-1 was also developed under von Braun. It was like a small pilotless airplane, 26 feet long, carrying a 1,900 pound warhead. Its buzzing engine stopped as it approached the target, whereupon the bomb would dive to the ground and explode. The first V-1s were launched in June 1944. From then until the Allies overran the last launch sites in March 1945, 6,000 people were killed and about 40,000 wounded, mostly in and around London. Some 32,000 were made by concentration camp prisoners, including a portion from the Mittelberg tunnels.

The V-2, the world's first large ballistic missile, was 46 feet long. It also carried a warhead of about one ton. It had a guidance system very advanced for the times, adequate for bombing urban areas, but not for pinpointing particular targets. It landed at 4,000 miles per hour, faster than the sound of its approach. If you heard the explosion, you were safe. The first V-2 attack on London occurred in early September 1944. Like the V-1s, V-2 attacks continued until March of the following year. V-2s accounted for almost 3,000 deaths and nearly 6,000 injuries in Britain. Many were launched against Antwerp as well, where several hundred were killed and many others injured.

The V-2 was the, "first man-made object to achieve suborbital spaceflight," and clearly represented the opening of a new dimension of strategic warfare. The rocket technology that it embodied was uniquely German. At the time, it was a spectacular and unsurpassed achievement, with obvious potential for future military development. Neither America nor any of its allies had anything like it. Both the Soviets and the Americans were quick to sequester all the able German technologists connected to these efforts that they could. Both obviously acted on the principle that the ends justified the means, a principle of action rarely advocated by philosophers, preachers or ethicists, nor acknowledged by most of its many practitioners.

END GAME

The Soviet Army was less than 100 miles from Peenemünde in the spring of 1945 when von Braun asked his planning staff to decide how and to whom they should surrender. *That* was an obvious no-brainer. Providentially, SS commander Kammler ordered von Braun's group to relocate to Mittelwerk soon after. An army chief ordered them to join the army and fight the approaching Russians. Von Braun and his associates chose Mittelwerk. Before long, with American forces closing in on Mittelwerk, Kammler selected von Braun and about 500 key engineers and other workers and ordered them relocated to the Bavarian Alps near Oberammergau. Reportedly, their SS guards had orders to execute them if they appeared about to fall into

American hands. Von Braun, however, suspected that Kammler was planning to hold them hostage as a personal bargaining chip with the Americans. He needed one of his own. On April 3, 1945, Von Braun dispatched a small team to bury fourteen tons of V-2 documents and plans in an abandoned salt mine near Mittelwerk. The team then blew up the roof of the mine. Its location was known only to a few.

On April 11, a week later, American forces arrived at nearby Nordhausen. To their amazement they soon discovered the immense abandoned underground factory, electricity still turned on, thousands of dead bodies littering the grounds outside, a few living skeletons lying helpless among the dead or wandering in the shadows. However, British forces were scheduled to occupy the region soon, replacing the Americans. The Americans rushed into action. Within three weeks they had shipped 341 rail cars loaded with V-2 parts for 100 V-2 rockets to Antwerp where they sailed off to America on sixteen Liberty ships just days before the British took over. British protests that the U.S. had agreed to turn over half the V-2s to them were ignored. By mid-May an American major had tricked one of von Braun's key men into revealing the location of the hidden papers, without which the V-2 hardware would have been next to useless. In late May, only hours before the British occupied the area where the papers were buried, the last of the stolen papers were retrieved and shipped off to the Aberdeen Proving Ground in Maryland.

Meanwhile, on May 2, 1945, von Braun's brother, riding a bicycle near Obergammerau, encountered a private from advancing American forces, and in broken English, told him his name, said his brother had invented the V-2, and that they wanted to surrender. The Americans took them all to Garmish-Partenkirchen for interrogation. On May 3, 1945, one month after Hans Kammler had ordered the von Braun team transported to the south, two days before Russian troops reached Peenemünde, von Braun can be seen posing with U.S. troops to whom he had just surrendered. The Army soon offered a one-year contract to von Braun and 127 members of his team under what was known as Operation Paperclip. They were among the first "Paperclip" Germans to come to the U.S.

OPERATION PAPERCLIP

Operation Paperclip led, over a period of years, to the immigration of some 1,600 Germans—mostly rocket engineers and experts, with some family members—who had served the Nazi regime and would bring their technical and scientific expertise with them. Records disclosing their Nazi affiliations and responsibilities, von Braun's included, were duly classified "secret" by the Army.

When the Paperclip project was revealed to the public around the middle of 1945, my mother was appalled. How, she demanded, could the authorities even think about bringing these men, who had worked their hearts out for Hitler, to the United States? It was a moral disgrace. No practical advantage could, in her view, counterbalance the immorality of overlooking, and thus effectively condoning the evils these people had actively helped implement. However, official expediency, moral indifference and bureaucratic cover-up trumped all that. Alas! I doubt that my mother would have invited von Braun to dinner.

In this country, von Braun rose rapidly through ability and persistence and extraordinary adaptability. By 1950 he had become chief of guided missile development at the Army's Redstone Arsenal near Huntsville, Alabama. In 1955 he became a U.S. citizen. Three years later, as noted earlier, he was on the cover of TIME. Two years after that, in 1960, his entire operation was transferred to NASA, America's National Aeronautics and Space Agency, newly created in 1958 after Sputnik 1 and its successors. The Huntsville operation was renamed the Marshall Space Flight Center, with Von Braun, at the head of 5,000 people, its Director. He was already the most famous personality in the U.S. space program. Now he was one of NASA's most prominent officials, a distinguished leader in its stirring mission: the exploitation of space for peaceful purposes on behalf of the United States and all mankind.

VON BRAUN COMES TO DINNER

Not long after, I met him in the Pentagon where he appeared on a visit to Washington. As I have said, we had never met. I invited him to our home for dinner. He accepted graciously. I thought my kids—Angela was only about 4 years old, William 8, (Robert, 16, was away at school)—would be thrilled to have dinner with Wernher von Braun. The Wheaties box was usually on their breakfast table. Now he himself would be at the dinner table.

Von Braun was about 48 years old, eight years older than I was. Needless to say, this first meeting could not be an occasion for asking the honored guest about his Nazi past. I remember it as a pleasant encounter with one of the country's most prominent and accomplished technology leaders, a particularly charming and attractive man, to which could be added the charisma that attended him as a famous public figure. Contrary to my expectations, however, the evening was marred by the indifference of the children to the great man's presence. Angela fell asleep at the table. William took no noticeable interest in von Braun. I was disappointed. It crossed my mind that the aristocratic von Braun would consider their behavior a sign of poor breeding. I was inclined to agree with his imagined judgment. I never saw von Braun again.

Soon after, in the spring of 1961, President Kennedy led the U.S. into the conquest of space. On May 8 he announced his intention to support Project Apollo, committed to the goal of sending men on a round-trip to the moon within a decade. The Marshall center, under von Braun's direction, became responsible for developing the giant Saturn V launch vehicle that would propel the astronauts into lunar orbit. The V-2 rocket, of which he had been in charge more than twenty years before, had been 46 feet long. Saturn V was 363 feet long, one-quarter the height of the Empire State building. In its final form it consisted of three stages weighing nearly seven million pounds. It had a payload capacity of 260,000 pounds. At take-off it shook the ground 50 miles away.

No other launch vehicle ever surpassed it in height, weight, payload or reliability. It had no failures. It operated repeatedly and perfectly in outer space. Unquestionably, Saturn V was the most powerful, complex and correspondingly successful rocket development of all time, and remains so to this day. Its cost is a partial measure of its complexity. The Manhattan Project that produced the first atomic bombs cost $23 billion in 2007 dollars. While direct comparisons are only approximate, Saturn V certainly cost about as much, and probably cost more

TRANSFORMATIONS

In his native Germany, von Braun was a Lutheran, a Nazi and an SS officer, who knew and was known by Hitler, Himmler, Speer and every major military chief. In America, he was none of those. "He became a Born-Again and joined the congregation of a small Church of the Nazarene in Texas." Later in his ascendancy here he became a more fashionable Episcopalian. He worked for the American Army, became Deputy Associate Administrator of NASA, and spent a few years as a vice-president of Fairchild Industries. He knew and was known by Presidents Eisenhower, Kennedy and Johnson, and was long an idolized favorite on Capitol Hill.

He identified himself as a Creationist, and provided numerous conversational clues and some public utterances in support of his close identification with religious teaching and piety. The Internet abounds with Lutheran and other religious sites recording saccharine testimonials to von Braun's conviction of the omnipresence of God, the authority of the Bible and his devotion to morality and his fellow man. The quality of his recorded utterances on these matters is reflected in the following:

> While technology controls the forces of nature around us, ethics try to control the forces of nature within us . . . I think it is a fair assumption that the Ten Commandments are entirely adequate— without amendments—to cope with all the problems the technological revolution not only has brought up, but will bring in the future. The real problem is not a lack of ethical legislation, but a lack in day-to-day guidance and control. . . . When science freed itself from the bonds of religious dogma, thus opening the way for the technological revolution, the Church also lost much of its influence on the ethical conduct of man.

Von Braun seems to have forgotten some five or six centuries during which, exemplifying aspects of the Church's "influence on the ethical conduct of man," the victims of Inquisitorial convictions were routinely burned alive as the Church offered holy incentives to worshippers bringing faggots for the fires. Still, publics being what they are, his public image appears in some quarters to have benefited substantially from such utterances and writings.

Time passed. The contrasts that illuminate his unique trajectory through life gave rise to volumes of satire and caricature among those less susceptible to rock-star allure. Many thought that Dr. Strangelove was, however improbably, a caricature of von Braun. Tom Lehrer's satirical verse says volumes:

Gather round while I sing you of Wernher von Braun,
A man whose allegiance is ruled by expedience;
Call him a Nazi, he won't even frown,
"Ha, Nazi schmazi," says Wernher von Braun.

Don't say that he's hypocritical,
Say rather that he's apolitical.
"Once the rockets are up, who cares where they come down?
"That's not my department," says Wernher von Braun.

Some have harsh words for this man of renown,
But some think our attitude should be one of gratitude,
Like the widows and cripples in old London town,
Who owe their large pensions to Wernher von Braun.

You too may be a big hero,
Once you've learned to count backwards to zero,
"In German oder English I know how to count down,
"Und I'm learning Chinese," says Wernher von Braun.

MEMORIES FADE, GHOSTS RISE

Plenty of German scientists and engineers did what they could to end up in American hands as the war drew to a close. Many were not successful and spent years in Russia where, like their Paper Clip counterparts in America, they plied their craft in behalf of their former enemy. Eventually the Soviets decided they had learned everything the Germans had to teach, whereupon most were repatriated to Germany.

In contrast, those who came to America settled here. They formed families, bought houses, became citizens and, in numerous cases, earned recognition and held top jobs. Von Braun, like most of them, spent less than a third of his working life in Germany and the rest in the United States. More than any other among them, or any American "rocket scientist," he rose rapidly as a visionary, a consummate engineer, an exceptional leader and, uniquely, the most familiar icon of the burgeoning Space Age in its years of infancy and rapid growth. He would never entirely outlive his shadowing past in Nazi Germany, but it remained little more than that, a modest shadow during his lifetime, before documented and eye-witness records of his clouded past came to light.

Today, nearly five decades later, national memory and interest in all this has largely faded away. Almost half the U.S. population has been born since von Braun died in 1977 at the age of 65. Nobody born after 1960 has a clear memory of von Braun's Wheaties Box fame. The space race in which, as it turned out, the Soviets never ran, vanished from public consciousness after the moon landings. Already, even before his greatest achievement, my children's attention wandered, and one of them fell asleep, as he sat at our table. They, and other millions from that era, are in their fifties and sixties now.

The conquest of space and its one-time heroes became subjects of history, while a corresponding interest in the writings of survivors and in unearthing discomfiting, hidden or long-classified records of the profound moral contamination afflicting some of its principal German architects, grew. One result became the case of Arthur Rudolph, the Saturn V project director under von Braun.

THE CASE OF ARTHUR RUDOLPH

In 1982 the Office of Special Investigations (OSI) opened an investigation of Rudolph's past. By then he was retired in San Jose, California. Almost 80 years old, he had had triple-by-pass surgery. He had been an American citizen since 1954. The Army had awarded him the Exceptional Civilian Service Medal. NASA had awarded him both the Exceptional and the Distinguished Service Medal. A local university had awarded him an honorary PhD degree. Why Rudolph? Why now?

Under von Braun in Germany he had been Chief Production Engineer of the Peenemünde V-2 assembly facility. It was Rudolph, as noted earlier, who in 1943 had visited the Heinkel aircraft plant where concentration camp labor was being used on a large scale (as it was by dozens of leading German companies such as Heinkel, Junkers, BMW, Siemens, Bayer, I.G. Farben, Krupp and many others, some of these at Dora.) When, after the British bombed Peenemünde in August 1943, it was decided to move production to the abandoned gypsum tunnels near Nordhausen, a move approved by Hitler and the notorious SS Chief Heinrich Himmler, The Mittelwerk Company was incorporated the next month; a contract for 12,000 V-2s was signed; SS. Gen. Hans Kammler was put in charge; and Arthur Rudolph was dispatched to Mittelwerk with several hundred Peenemünde staff, to oversee the technical side of V-2 production. He remained there until just before the region was overrun by the American army about eighteen months later. The ghastly horrors of the Mittelwerk-Dora-Nordhausen complex have already been briefly recounted. Rudolph was involved at a policy and a working level from the start.

The answer to *Why now?*—why a retired old man in ill health, an American citizen with a splendid record decades long, was targeted by the U.S. government for his Nazi past, one shared with many other Paperclip immigrants, begins when, in 1979, 34 years after Operation Paperclip had begun, the U.S. Congress opened an investigation to uncover Nazi war criminals living in the U.S. The OSI pursued Rudolph on the basis of his own voluntary testimony, given without legal counsel. Only years later, after these investigations, would Rudolph's complicity in introducing forced labor to Peenemünde in 1943 come to light. Effectively, Rudolph, now far beyond any use to the space or any other program, was coerced into surrendering his American citizenship with threats against his family, his NASA pension and his social security income.

Still, there was little question that he was implicated with Nazi atrocities. So was von Braun, except that he had died in 1977, and this was years later. After a year of negotiating with the OSI, Rudolph was forced to face prosecution or leave the country, which he did in 1983. A mix of neo-Nazis, Pat Buchanan, the notorious Lyndon LaRouche, and others of similar ilk, leapt to his defense. Congressmen gave speeches proposing special punitive legislation against Rudolph. Eventually, his case was reviewed by the West German government. Failing to discover or choosing to ignore Rudolph's early advocacy for using forced labor to manufacture V-2s or his close connections with the ghastly consequences at Mittelwerk-Dora, he was granted German citizenship. He died there a dozen years later in 1996, deeply resentful of his ungrateful treatment by America.

It seems unlikely, given the organizational and popular status he achieved, that von Braun, had he lived, would have been subject to the treatment that befell Rudolph. Indeed, according to a recent biography, "One of the investigators of the Rudolph case said, 'We're lucky von Braun isn't alive.' If he had been, he might well have defended Rudolph successfully." As it was, von Braun died in a timely manner, his decades of transient fame still intact, five years before the blinding light of investigative zeal shone on shadows a half-century old.

But then, already nearly fifty years ago, my children fell asleep, or drifted into visible inattention, in von Braun's presence. Little by little, so far as von Braun's former fame is concerned, at least half of America has already dozed off. Some of the rest of us, especially those who were his near-contemporaries, with few more years to go, remember.

THE MORAL LAW WITHIN?

Emmanuel Kant wrote "Two things fill the mind with ever new and increasing admiration and awe, the more often and steadily we meditate upon them: the starry firmament above and the moral law within." One obvious meditation is that the same stars shine on everyone, while the "moral law within" offers fewer and rather less awe-inspiring objects for universal admiration. Von Braun's trajectory through life inspires reflection on such matters.

The moral law within him, as it is for everyone, was and is defined not by what he claimed to believe, but by his distortions, his evasions, his silences and above all, his acts. He yearned from early youth to break the bounds of Earth and fly to the starry firmament above. The V-1, the V-2, Nordhausen/Dora and, decades later, the Apollo rocket (Saturn V), were among his signal legacies.

Wernher von Braun is buried in the Ivy Hill cemetery in Alexandria, Virginia. His small headstone displays only his name, the dates of his birth and death, and "Psalms 19:1" inscribed below the latter. According to the King James translation it reads:

The heavens declare the glory of God, and the firmament sheweth his handiwork.

Who does not recall the startling brilliance of a falling star that flames upon the night? Who long remarks thereafter the stars it blinded or the darkness from which it came?

PARTIAL BIBLIOGRAPHY

Encyclopedia of the Holocaust. Macmillan Publishing Company, New York. Collier Macmillan Publishers, London. 1990. See especially articles on Buchenwald and Dora-Nordhausen.

Neufeld, Michael J. Von Braun, *Dreamer Of Space—Engineer Of War*. Alfred A. Knopf, New York 2008. 587 pages. The most recent and authoritative biography of von Braun. An excellent and comprehensive treatment.

Mittelwerk.
http://en.wikipedia.org/wiki/Mittelwerk.

A very brief summary of the underground WWII rocket and aircraft factory complex. The summary includes a brief description of the role of Mittelwerk GmBH, the chief production goals, the deaths of thousands of prisoners, and a few other signal facts. It is by no means comprehensive or complete.

Mittelwerk/Mittelbau/Camp Dora Mittelbau GmBH-Mittelbau KZ.
www.v2rocket.com/start/chapters/mittel.html. Sixteen pages.

Excellent summary of the founding of the facilities, their initial construction by prisoners from Buchenwald, projects other than V-2 production, the gruesome statistics and description of the operation of the Dora camp and its many satellites, all of them death camps, working conditions, abandonment by the Germans, the barbaric evacuation of prisoners, the final escape of the von Braun team, how the Americans spirited away most of the useful missile hardware remaining, von Braun's surrender to American forces.

Wernher von Braun; Walter Dornberger; Magnus von Braun; Peenemünde; Arthur Rudolf; Saturn V; Hans Kammler; and related subjects may be found on the Internet.

5

CURTIS LeMAY

I arrived in the Pentagon in early 1959 to begin serving under Dr. Herbert F. York as Assistant Director of Defense Research and Engineering. York was the first director of this new office established by the Defense Reorganization Act of 1958, enacted in the aftermath of Soviet Sputnik space spectaculars that began with the first-ever artificial earth satellite in October 1957. The Director, an under-Secretary in rank, was responsible for "supervising all research and engineering in the Defense Establishment." I was charged with "strategic weapons"—mostly bombers and long-range missiles—and although procedures remained to be worked out in the months ahead, I was the first link in the chain, followed by York, and finally the Secretary of Defense, of approval or disapproval of any proposed strategic military weapon system.

Soon after I arrived, Herb asked me to listen to an Air Force proposal for a new development called the ALBM (Air Launched Ballistic Missile), later to be called Skybolt. Its stated purpose was to develop a ballistic missile that would be launched in the air from B-52 bombers at Soviet ground-to-air defenses up to 1,000 miles away. These defenses, so the story went, would be knocked out by ALBMs so that the bombers could more safely proceed to drop bombs on Soviet strategic targets. It was a proposal of enormous complexity and dubious feasibility. That first briefing led to my first meeting with the famous General Curtis LeMay, then the Air Force vice-Chief of Staff.

The day for the presentation came. I had given countless briefings to military audiences during the past fifteen years, but the military had never given a briefing to me. Now, as I walked into the small conference room, I found a customary situation curiously reversed. At the end of the room a colonel was setting up the familiar easel with its mass of large flip-charts affixed to it—laptops and power-point presentations lay decades in the future.

To my surprise, the room was half-filled with uniformed Air Force officers who accompanied the briefer but contributed nothing but their stolid presence. I, all by myself, was the intended audience. It was my first of many such experiences. I never understood why so many non-participants appeared at these sessions. None of them said a word. None were introduced. If their presence was intended to intimidate the outnumbered Defense Department listener, it never worked on me. The Colonel began. His top chart identified the briefing subject: the ALBM—a ballistic missile to be launched from a bomber in flight.

I had known about the Hound Dog cruise missile project for more than ten years. It, too, was to be carried under the wings of long-range bombers. Indeed, the first production Hound Dog was to be delivered only nine months after the briefing I was about to hear. Each of two Hound Dogs was to be armed with a 1.5 megaton atomic bomb. Two of them greatly exceeded the TNT equivalent of all the bombs dropped by the Allies in all the years of WWII in both the European and Pacific theaters, if not in all prior human history.

Hound Dog's military purpose was identical to that of the proposed ALBM. Hound Dog, however, suffered a major drawback: it was not a *ballistic* missile. It flew like a small plane. The ALBM, by contrast, was a giant rocket guided for a short time as it rose into space, supposed to hit its distant target on its fall to earth.

In 1959, *ballistic* was the wave of the future. In early 1960 the Air Force Chief Gen. Tommy White announced a new project, SKYBOLT at the Washington Press Club podium. It was headline news, although in reality, simply a better-sounding name for the unapproved ALBM project which by the time he spoke had been awaiting approval for nearly a year. Gen. White reportedly declared, off the record, that "if the Navy can launch a ballistic missile from a submarine, we can launch one from a bomber." But: back to the ALBM briefing, where these approaching realities still lay beyond the political horizon.

The second chart was a cartoon-like sketch showing a mushroom cloud above the inscription: "Atomic Bombs Are Powerful." The rest was almost equally absurd. The chief revelation was that the Air Force had already signed a contract with Douglas Aircraft as prime contractor. They were asking for money, not project approval.

I was not quite clear about what I was supposed to do about it. Procedures in place were not yet geared to the role and powers of the newly installed ODDR&E (Office of the Director of Defense Research and Engineering). Its operations had just begun. I reflected on these circumstances in a mid-1970 interview for the John F. Kennedy Library:

> When this was all over I talked to Herb [York] about it a little bit. "It just shocks me," I said, "that they would come and give a briefing like that to a responsible official." He said, "You'd better do something about that,"

so I got all the correspondence and began to write letters to them. I soon discovered that they were really very serious about and determined to preserve this process, of which giving ODR&E [our office] the idiot treatment was only a part. The process was the weapons system acquisition process of the late fifties and early sixties.

You, the Air Force, for example, decided that the time had come to start a new weapon system, but you were not exactly sure what it would or should be like, so you talked to some contractors about it, either formally or informally. Then you engaged in a very superficial process for selecting a prime contractor.

The briefer had outlined how Douglas Aircraft had been selected as the prime contractor. He listed many subcontractors already earmarked for the ALBM team.

So you put these elements together and then got somebody to approve the "project" which had no specifications that meant anything, no schedules that meant anything, no budgets that meant anything, none of the control mechanisms that are commonplace today in weapons system procurement, nothing. Once approved you signed a letter contract and then the contractor would proceed to organize a team of people. Oftentimes contractors spent substantial sums in anticipation of a contract, recouping such costs when the contract was signed.

So I withheld approval. Instead, I required Douglas Aircraft to submit a number of studies and plans without which no multi-million dollar project should be started. The next couple of months were taken up with specifying the preliminary work to be done, visiting Douglas (Donald Douglas Sr., the aviation pioneer still running the company, spoke with me at length on several occasions), being visited repeatedly by the young project manager in charge of the ALBM at Douglas, pleading for approval, and studying documents that the company submitted.

When I arrived at the Pentagon I discovered that an aide, Dr. Max Oldham, had been assigned to me. He had spent a few years working for the Air Force as a civilian analyst. There he had come to know Gen. Curtis LeMay. Now, mid-1959, LeMay was the Air Force vice-Chief of Staff under Gen. Thomas White. One day, a few months after the ALBM briefing, Oldham suggested that the time had come for me to meet Gen. LeMay.

I was new to the Pentagon and unpracticed in the arts of bureaucratic maneuver and paranoia, so it never occurred to me that Max Oldham had probably been in frequent touch with Le May for the past few months, that he had probably explained that I was standing in the way of ALBM funding, and that LeMay had probably told Oldham to get Rubel up there to his office so we can get this thing going. I took Dr. Oldham at his word—sure, I should meet LeMay—so, in a couple of days, off we marched to LeMay's spacious office on the fifth floor of the Pentagon.

LeMay was one of the most famous generals of WWII. Most of them had faded away fairly fast after the war. Not LeMay. His fame and accomplishments continued for years after the war ended. We first heard of him when the B-17 Flying Fortress mass bombing raid he led on the Schweinfurt-Regensburg mission over Germany in August 1943 made national headlines. Reportedly, 42% of Germany's ball bearing production was located in and around Schweinfurt, and this daring raid had crippled it. It was a big raid on a comparatively small city. It included hundreds of planes, including 376 B-17s. LeMay himself organized and flew on this mission.

What the papers did not recount were the catastrophic losses that made a swift follow-up attack by our decimated forces impossible.

Only months later did a second and equally famous attack on Schweinfurt finally take place, equally if not more costly to the attackers. Only thirty three bombers landed without damage, and nearly sixty were shot down. Still, I and millions of other newspaper readers remembered Schweinfurt as a massive, daring and putatively successful strike against German ball bearing plants. Until near the end of the European phase of WWII the Army Air Force repeatedly declared that it did not engage in what the British called "terror bombing." The United States tactic was "precision bombing" against strategic (i.e.: war-making capacities far behind the ground-war front.) The Schweinfurt raids were supposed to be examples.

A year after those raids, LeMay was transferred to the Pacific theater in command of all strategic air operations against the Japanese home islands. The weather conditions over Japan were markedly different from those in Europe. Bombing accuracy from high altitudes flying over persistent cloud cover was severely degraded. Japanese air defenses inflicted unsustainable losses. What ensued under LeMay's command was the most savage campaign of terror bombing of WWII.

LeMay radically revised bomber tactics. Now bombers were to fly at night at seemingly suicidal altitudes as low as 5,000 feet. As the British had done for years, LeMay's bombers would drop incendiary bombs on some sixty-four Japanese cities, lighting the way in each raid to successive waves of both incendiary and high-explosive bombings. In a massive raid on Tokyo in March 1945, nearly 2,000 tons of incendiary bombs were dropped in a three-hour period. More than 100,000 civilians were killed. 250,000 buildings and 16 square miles of Tokyo were burned down. Nobody knows for sure, but estimates run up to a million Japanese civilians killed in U.S. air raids between March and August 1945, when the war ended. Other studies suggest that 30%-50% of the inhabitants of the largely defenseless cities attacked by our bombers were killed in air raids, and that some 8.5 million survivors were left homeless. LeMay "was quite aware of both the brutality of his actions and the Japanese opinion of him—he once remarked that had the U.S. lost the war, he fully expected to be tried for war crimes."

LeMay was the youngest general officer in the Army Air Force when he was promoted during WWII. He was the youngest four-star general in U.S. military history except for Ulysses S. Grant. After commanding the post-war 1948 Berlin Airlift that broke the back of the Soviet's cold-war blockade of Berlin, he became the father of the Strategic Air Command (SAC). More than any other military figure apart from Dwight Eisenhower, LeMay had been in the public eye all my working life, from the 1943 Schweinfurt raids to the day I first met him in 1959.

I, on the other hand, had spent essentially my entire anonymous post-graduate life in development laboratories. Now I was charged with overlooking all military strategic weapon developments. No doubt LeMay thought he knew a lot about what I knew, and that I knew little or nothing about what he knew. I already had some of these notions in mind when, on the appointed day, Dr. Oldham introduced me to Gen. LeMay in his spacious office, then left. LeMay shook my hand and pointed to a large, cushioned, leather-covered club chair facing his desk. I sat down. He sat behind his desk, chewing on his signature cigar, staring at me, saying nothing. He was fifty-two years old with square, craggy features and a full head of iron-gray hair. Central casting could not have found a more fitting person to portray LeMay than LeMay himself.

Lincoln Steffens, a muckraking reporter from the early part of the twentieth century, recounts in his autobiography how one of the big city bosses he interviewed had been the master of intimidating silence, saying nothing while his visitor became increasingly uncomfortable. I remembered that, sitting in the awkward silence, trading stares with the famous general, who sat behind his ample desk clamping his cigar, saying nothing. I decided that he was the senior man, I was in his office, that it was up to him to speak first, and that I could stare at him just as long as he could stare at me. So I relaxed into the comforting folds of the over-stuffed armchair, looking the much-decorated general squarely in the eye, watching him watch me. Finally, he gave in. Slowly and deliberately he took the cigar out of his mouth, leaned forward over his large, dark mahogany desk, his shoulders hunched into his chest, and slowly growled in a low, gravely tone: "The trouble is, there are too goddam many civilians **messing around** with military affairs they don't know a **goddam thing about**." With that he put the cigar back between his teeth and leaned back in his swiveled, high-back judge's chair, still staring at me. It was a statement, not a question. I said nothing, still looking into his eyes.

After another long, expectant delay, he leaned forward again, cigar once more between two fingers, and went on. "There's nothing wrong with civilians doing things for the military that the military needs. I started RAND (an early think-tank under Air Force auspices) after the war to figure out what weapon systems were going to be needed by the fighting man. That's what RAND was for, to help get weapons into the hands of the fighting man. Now they want to tell us how to run a war." He drawled w-a-a-h-r. "That's what R&D is all about, to put weapons into the hands of the fighting man. The trouble is, the people who are supposed to do that don't know anything about the needs of the fighting man. Take YOU, for example. They tell me that you are holding up the ALBM. That's a weapon the fighting man needs. We need that weapon in SAC. You ought to know something about SAC. You ought to know what the fighting man needs. What about that—you ever been to SAC?"

At last LeMay had asked a question. I replied that, yes, I had just returned from a week at SAC, that I had gone through high-altitude indoctrination and flown on a Headstart mission with live H-bombs (a 24-hour non-stop flight from northwestern bases across Canada, refueling over Labrador, to the Arctic Circle and back.) I had toured headquarters, been given many briefings and met twice with the SAC commander, General Power. I said I was mightily impressed by my visit to SAC. "You might say," I added, "that I have been SACUMCISED."

I suppose he had heard that one before. Still, LeMay sank back into his chair in a visibly more relaxed posture. The hint of a smile crossed his face for a brief moment. I turned to the ALBM matter. "You say I am holding up the ALBM. What I **have** done is show how ill-prepared the contractor is to be given the go-ahead." I asked him if he knew how much had already been spent on the ALBM for nothing more than some basic studies critical to any successful project. He said he didn't.

"About $10 million," I said. "And do you know what you've got for your money?" I asked. He said he didn't. I pointed to some papers on his desk. "See those papers on your desk? You have ALBM reports from Douglas about as thick as that thin pile. Do you know what they are worth?" He looked quizzical. "About as much as the paper they are printed on," I said. With that LeMay became positively voluble. He knew it, he knew it, those defense contractors don't know how to manage. SAC knows how to manage. Those aerospace companies, those contractors definitely are a problem, he avowed. They can't manage.

I was to have many contacts with LeMay in the years to come. He was a tough manager and a fierce advocate for the Air Force, especially for bomber forces and SAC. He represented a deep-dyed military attitude that, in him, was distinguished by an attractive candor, although nobody I ever knew agreed with his often egregious opinions.

Within a couple of months of arriving at the Pentagon, as I was digging into details of the critical strategic weapon systems,

I discovered what turned out to be a major flaw in the provisions for controlling the launch of Minuteman missiles. More than a thousand were ultimately deployed. This is not the place to describe some of the system's complex but critical details. Suffice it to say that the most unimaginable catastrophe in history could hang on a single command and the obedience of no more than four young Air Force airmen in underground Minuteman launch silos somewhere out in the plains of North Dakota. That would be all it took to launch the fifty missiles in each squadron. Fifty missiles would deliver about 15 *megatons* of TNT-equivalent atomic warheads, roughly equivalent to six times the high-explosive bombs dropped on all theaters in WWII, and globally radioactive in addition. There were no options. To launch or not to launch meant all the squadron's missiles, or none, an electro-mechanical necessity. The system was *designed* this way on purpose.

I quickly discovered that while the Minuteman launch system was even more complex and dangerous than I at first realized, it was symptomatic of the more embracing problem of command and control of strategic weapons generally. This became one of my chief concerns for the next several years. One day, when command and control had become a major Administration and Defense concern, I mentioned the subject to Gen. LeMay. The matter came up as I stood facing the general as he stood across from me at his desk. Somehow, in the context of a wholly different subject, I must have uttered the term "command and control."

LeMay expostulated contemptuously: "Command and control! Command and control! What's that? It's telling the fighting man what to do, that's what it is. And that's a job for the professional soldier. They talk about the president exercising command and control. What is the president?" He spit out the "p" in president. "A politician." He spit out the "p" in "politician." "What does a politician know about war?" He dwelled on w-a-a-h-r. "Who needs the president if there's a w-a-a-h r? Nobody! All we need him for is to tell us that there *is* a war. We are professional soldiers. We'll take care of the rest.[1]"

I had learned a few things in the two years or so since my first encounter with LeMay. This particular comment sharply summarized a point of view going to the very heart of Eisenhower's warnings about the creeping dangers of "powers, sought and unsought," both of a "military-industrial complex" and a "scientific, technological elite" in the contemporary world. It marks a critical divide between the military that designs, develops, deploys and directly controls American military weapons on the one hand, and those—the President, specifically, and through him, his senior officers—who hold the sole Constitutional power and responsibility to command, on the other. Besides, it is a viewpoint entirely unsupported by the history of real wars, of which Churchill's indispensable and brilliant role is a leading but by no means the sole example. (Cohen 1967)

On another occasion, LeMay reacted with exceptional vigor when I used the term "limited war" in a passing comment. At the time, about 1962, the Vietnam war was escalating. He told me he had been asked to attend a meeting of some committee of the President's Science Advisory Committee. A recess was called. A few people, including LeMay, stayed at the table. He struck up a conversation with the scientist next to him. He asked him "How's it going?" The scientist—a *foreigner*—asked him, "General, how are you going to bomb those little brown men in Vietnam when you can't see them or anything else on the ground through the trees?"

LeMay's account was a study in the accents of contumely. *Foreigner* dripped with disdain. Not that LeMay was unfamiliar with "foreigners." The revered Theodore von Kármán had been a major Air Force advisor and chairman of the USAF Science Advisory Committee for many years. The only "foreigner" on the PSAC at the time that came to my mind was George Kistiakowsky, formerly Eisenhower's science advisor, who, along with Johnny von Neumann, another "foreigner," was the principal architect of the implosion lens system used in Fat Man (and subsequent plutonium bombs), the second atomic bomb, exploded over Nagasaki. LeMay, who prided himself on his earlier roles in promoting Air Force research and development, must have known, and surely valued, the roles of many other leading foreigners, among them Hans Bethe, Eugene Wigner, Enrico Fermi, Johnny von Neumann, Stan Ulam, Edward Teller and Wernher von Braun.

But, LeMay went on to recount, his conversation with "those people" was of no use. Look at North Korea, he said, another example of "limited war." Instead of bringing on the B-52s and getting the job done in Korea, war had raged up and down the land and ultimately laid it waste for miles and miles, far more devastated than a few massive, decisive bombing raids would have left it. Now it was happening in Vietnam, and nobody would listen to him.

Richard Rhodes had this to say about LeMay's vision of war:

> So LeMay's vision of war (and it's truly a horrific vision) was that we would launch everything we had, simultaneously, on early, early warning of a Soviet attack, maybe even a little before then, and would enter the Soviet Union from all sides at once, overwhelming their defenses (and he had plenty of evidence that it would overwhelm their defenses . . .), and simply take out the whole country at once. Nowhere in the documents that discuss these plans is there any discussion of the fact that you would kill 250 million people when you did that. That was just one of those collateral damage effects that you didn't discuss when you were laying such plans. . . . What did we think of the Nazis, that they killed 6 million Jews? What would the world think of democracy and of the United States of America if we had done such

a thing? Never mind the fact that the fallout from this killing of a nation would come back to us and kill most of us as well, even if nuclear winter didn't ensue. I think those are issues that must simply have been walled off from consideration, or I don't see how we could have done what we did. (Rhodes, 1986)

After further delays, and intense Air Force pressure, the ALBM, renamed for public relations reasons SKYBOLT, was allowed to proceed in early February, 1960. It ran into trouble almost at once. Technical problems I had anticipated early on loomed ever larger. In the event, they were never solved. A year later, John F. Kennedy was elected president. Robert McNamara became Secretary of Defense. As the new administration took over in early 1961, Skybolt development costs were rocketing. The program now involved the British in a complicated and politically charged venture which called for Skybolt to be developed by the Americans and then purchased by the British for their long-range V-bombers. Soon after Skybolt/ALBM funding was approved in early 1960, the British cancelled their Bluestreak long-range ballistic missile and lobbied frantically at the highest levels for Skybolt, upon which they now depended for their "independent nuclear deterrent," to be continued at all costs. But in the winter of 1962-63, the ax fell when McNamara (and Kennedy) cancelled Skybolt. All this, and the political repercussions, which led to the Skybolt Crisis, are described in the next chapter.

LeMay became the USAF chief of staff in 1961. His perspectives were often at odds with those of his political superiors. The 1962 Cuban Missile Crisis is an illustration:

Kennedy's resistance [to pressure from the military] reached a climax during the Cuban Missile Crisis. . . . The blockade or quarantine of Cuba that he imposed to force the removal of nuclear weapons did not satisfy the Joint Chiefs. When Kennedy first proposed it, General LeMay said he saw direct military intervention as a necessity. "This blockade and the political action I see leading into war," he told Kennedy in a conversation captured on tape by a White House recording device. "I don't see any other solution. It will lead right into war. This is almost as bad as the appeasement at Munich." LeMay indirectly threatened to make his dissent public. "I think that a blockade, and the political talk, would be considered by a lot of our friends and neutrals as being a pretty weak response to this. And I'm sure a lot of our own citizens would feel that way too. In other words, you're in a pretty bad fix at the present time."

LeMay's words angered Kennedy, who asked, "What did you say?" LeMay repeated: "You're in a pretty bad fix." Kenneth O'Donnell recalled in his memoirs that after the meeting, Kennedy asked him, "Can you imagine LeMay saying a thing like that? These brass hats have one great advantage in their favor. If we listen to them, and do what they want us to do, none of us will be alive later to tell them that they were wrong." (Kaplan, 2001.)

No doubt about it, LeMay did not mince words. Nor is there any doubt that he was a brilliant leader, a brilliant tactical innovator, a powerful advocate and skilled in maneuvering bureaucratic minefields. He won much and lost some. Where American military advice, ambitions and perceptions were trumped by scientific, technological or political realities, LeMay lost. Skybolt and the B-70 are leading examples. He did not fit well with Defense Secretary McNamara or Eugene Zuckert, USAF Secretary under McNamara, with President Kennedy, or with President Johnson. In 1965 he took retirement and moved to California. In 1968 he joined the campaign of George Wallace, the vividly racist former governor of Alabama, as candidate for vice-president on the American Independent Party ticket.

He had hoped to thwart Nixon's race for president, thinking him too conciliatory toward the Soviets. He was attacked as a racial bigot. LeMay, who had favored desegregating the armed forces in earlier years, ignored the campaign's racist coloration. His aggressive saber-rattling did not help the ticket. In the end, Wallace-LeMay won almost 14% of the popular vote, large enough to be a national disgrace, but far too small to win.

In the twenty-two years thereafter prior to his death at 84 in October 1990, LeMay was showered with honors from countries all over the world. Even the Japanese government, ironically enough, awarded him the First Order of Merit with the Grand Cordon of the Order of the Rising Sun. Even now, many web sites are devoted to his record and memory. I consulted one of these in the fall of 2006, where I counted some 115 notes honoring his 100th birthday on November 15. You can buy a copy of the Time Magazine cover of October 18, 1968, in a frame of your choice, on the Internet. It shows Wallace and LeMay as candidates graphically cartooned under the banner of THE REVOLT OF THE RIGHT. Both are eulogized in an American Daily site where their pro-war, anti-government, segregationist program is presented as a voice in American politics to which we should listen.

LeMay was a great military commander, innovative and, in many ways, brilliant, however limited his vision or dissonant his perspectives. He knew his own mind, and spoke it. That said, he was not fit for high office or excessive influence in the halls of power, from which he was eventually extruded. For some who recall him as he strode his hour upon the stage, his is a cautionary tale. For a vanishing coterie he remains an icon.

PARTIAL BIBLIOGRAPHY

Cohen, Eliot A. *Churchill at War,* Commentary, May 1967, pp.40-49.

Kaplan, Fred. JFK's First-Strike Plan. The Atlantic Monthly, October 2001.

Rhodes, Richard. *The Making of the Atomic Bomb,* Touchstone, Simon & Schuster, Inc, New York, 1986. For extended comments. See also: www.pbs.org/wbgh/amex/bomb.filmmore/reference/interview/rhodes07.html for this particular citation, which appears on numerous Internet sites.

6

THE SKYBOLT CRISIS

Eisenhower and Macmillan—March 1960

A few weeks after Skybolt funding was released in early February 1960, Harold Macmillan, the British prime minister, phoned President Eisenhower asking to meet with him. Momentous geopolitical matters were in the air. Unforeseen, the Soviets had yielded to Western demands for inspection rights at the Geneva nuclear test ban talks. Macmillan said he wanted to discuss nuclear test ban proposals. He said he thought this could be a "turning point in negotiations on disarmament." Without much enthusiasm, Eisenhower, scarcely able to refuse an old friend, agreed. Macmillan arrived in late March, but without his foreign secretary.

He had come primarily to negotiate a deal about Skybolt; he scarcely needed his foreign secretary for that. There had been lower-level talks about furnishing Polaris missiles and submarines to the British for their politically charged "independent nuclear deterrent," meaning a deterrent under their autonomous control, independent of NATO. Many in State and some in Defense opposed that on principle. Both State and Defense were against providing Polaris in any case. Defense Secretary Gates opposed offering Skybolt (he was promoting a NATO multilateral missile force), but State persuaded Defense to relent on Skybolt before Macmillan arrived.

One thing about this unusual happening appears pretty certain: the British prime minister knew a lot more about Skybolt than did the U.S. President at the time.[1] After all, Skybolt, funded for only a few weeks, was a larval program compared with the immense missile projects—Thor, Jupiter, Atlas, Titan, Polaris, some already deployed—that were far larger and of much greater national security importance. But as I knew from personal experience, the British were keenly interested in Skybolt even before it became a development project. A British liaison officer called on me often, starting right after my first briefing by the Air Force a year earlier, politely probing for hints about when final funding approval was likely. I was astonished to learn only after that briefing that British RAF officers had collaborated in writing the basic military "requirements" for Skybolt in 1958, and had sat in on the selection of Douglas Aircraft as the prime contractor early in 1959, a collaboration that American officials above the Air Force level, not to mention the President, apparently knew little or nothing about at the time. It would appear, however, that British collaboration in the Skybolt initiative was well known up to the top of the British government, perhaps from its early stages.

THE "CAMP DAVID" ACCORD

The President's briefing papers advised him to say that the U.S. would sell Skybolt to the British if and when it was successfully developed, and to make an implicit connection between that agreement and a British commitment to furnish berthing facilities for American Polaris submarines in the U.K. The discussions took place at Camp David, but also at intervals as the two leaders drove out to Eisenhower's farm in Pennsylvania to his son's home nearby, only part of the time in the presence of witnesses. Eisenhower and Macmillan each recorded his understanding of what had been agreed upon. Neither side initially accepted the other's version. An understanding was finally reached that stipulated that if the U.S. successfully developed Skybolt, it would sell production missiles to the U.K. "In the same spirit of cooperation," the British would make basing facilities available for U.S. Polaris submarines on the Clyde river, but there was no single version of this, nor any formal exchange of official documents. The two versions permitted and led to different interpretations, and different emphases on what had been agreed. Sometime during the next couple of years I secured a copy for my files.[2]

Macmillan returned to Britain and announced that the British Blue Streak intercontinental ballistic missile development was to be cancelled. Skybolt soon became an unremitting and growing political issue. About a month later, in late May, Harold Watkinson (then Minister of Defence) and Sir (later Lord) Solly Zuckerman, his Chief Scientific Advisor (CSA), flew to Washington to formalize a detailed agreement pursuant to the Eisenhower-Macmillan understanding. They met with Tom Gates, the U.S. Secretary of Defense at the time,[3] and then with me.

SOLLY ZUCKERMAN

I had already met with both Solly Zuckerman and Harold Watkinson in the U.K. Solly and I had hit it off well, and became and remained good friends until he died more than thirty years later. Solly lived in London during the week in a chic pied-a-terre.

Lady Joan, his wife, remained in their home in Birmingham, where Solly held the Sands Cox Chair in the Anatomy Department at the University of Birmingham. Joan was the grand-daughter of Rufus Isaacs, 1st Marquess of Reading, whose distinguished career included serving as Lord Chief Justice, Ambassador to the United States, and Viceroy of India. Solly, after studying medicine in South Africa, spent his early years studying physiology at Yale, Oxford and Birmingham. By 1943 he had been elected to the Fellowship of the Royal Society in recognition of his research on primate behavior and its physiological basis, especially the role of sex hormones.[4]

I was a guest at the Zuckerman home in Birmingham on several occasions. In London Solly often took me to lunch or dinner at the Atheneum or Brooks, and was often our guest in Washington, where he customarily consumed the better part of a bottle of champagne before dinner. Years later, when both he and I had retired, my wife, Robin, and I spent several days with him and Joan in their Norfolk home. Solly was deceivingly laid back and self-effacing. When he was elevated to a life peerage a year or so after we first met he took the title of Baron Zuckerman of Burnham Thorpe, the village where he lived in his later years. He was to be addressed as Solly (not Lord) Zuckerman, he told me, because his lifelong identity, his role, as it were, was "Solly."

As the collection of his writings and multiple associations reveals, he kept many balls in the air at the same time without appearing to do so. In the crush of his duties as the CSA for Defence he continued to oversee the London Zoo, to remain as head of his Birmingham department of anatomy, and to publish his *A New System of Anatomy* in 1961, a splendidly lucid and well-illustrated work, a copy of which he gave me in February 1962.

Solly's many activities, his scientific reputation and his many contacts in the United States did not work entirely to his advantage in Ministry of Air and RAF circles. At a 2007 gathering of British officials and intellectuals who had served in the early 1960s, a participant recalled how members of the British Air Force became "immensely indignant when there came to notice some indication that Solly Zuckerman had conveyed to the Americans that we wouldn't mind all that much if [Skybolt] was scrubbed."[5] I had far more contact with Solly over many years than did anyone else in the U.S. at the time. He never made any such intimations to me, and I doubt that he made them to anyone else, but his connections in America aroused suspicions in the Defence circles for whom Skybolt was seen as the only way to extend the life of the British bomber fleet, the only acceptable way to perpetuate their independent deterrent, and a solemn obligation of the Americans to develop, produce, and sell to the U.K. Besides, both the U.S. and U.K. Air Forces were focused on arguments over technical feasibility—would the guidance system work, or was the missile steering system practical—never upon Skybolt's utility in the context of vast ballistic missile developments and deployments.

However, Solly was not and never pretended to be up on the engineering problems afflicting the Skybolt concept. Indeed, he wrote, surprisingly, that the U.K. did not "have 'experts' to match John Rubel or Jerry Wiesner in assessing the technical feasibility of the Skybolt concept as a whole,"[6] implicitly recusing himself out of an excess of modesty. The British had experts, all right, but few or none were sufficiently detached from bomber die-hards, or from ties to the USAF and the Skybolt project itself, to assert a needed objectivity.

It may be said, however, that despite his many scientific achievements, Solly was sometimes conspicuously incurious when it came to modest technical details. As we entered his Birmingham house on my first visit there, Solly said that perhaps he should raise the temperature to better accord with my "American taste." Outside, a heavy mist left a film of moisture on every leaf and blade of grass under cold, damp, gray skies, utterly miserable weather, especially for one accustomed to the more agreeable climate of Southern California. Inside the house it was almost as cold.

However, Solly went on, it would not do any good to turn the thermostat up because the heating system only worked from 6 PM until 10 PM. We would have to wait two hours before the thermostat would have any effect. Why? Because, he said, that was how the system worked. I asked to see the furnace. A timing device was in plain sight. Two little moveable tabs were lightly screwed to the periphery of its rotating clock disk. I reset the start time to 4 PM. When I asked Solly why he didn't just remove the tabs and set the thermostat wherever he wanted it whenever he wished, he said he didn't know.

1960–1961

Defence Minister Harold Watkinson and Solly arrived in Washington about a month after the Camp David agreement. Watkinson got Gates to approve a draft "memorandum of understanding" governing detailed technical and financial arrangements for Skybolt. After meeting with Gates they met with me. I told them, as Solly later wrote, that "the project was a very speculative one. . . It would be some time before the United States could decide whether Skybolt was a reality, and in consequence it was far too early for a government-to-government 'contract to purchase.'" [7]

Macmillan met with them immediately upon their return, eager to know what had happened. He was particularly pleased to learn that Watkinson thought he had "successfully disassociated the British Government from the [American] notion that a submarine base in Scotland should be a quid pro quo for Skybolt" as Macmillan and Eisenhower had appeared to agree not long before. This was only the first British attempt to "interpret" the Camp David agreement, this time as a way to avoid granting berthing rights to Polaris submarines in the U.K. That posture, as we shall see, was soon reversed.[8]

By now, Skybolt and the related matter of Holy Loch had become a chiefly political matter. British opponents of American nuclear submarines on the Clyde feared they would make the U.K. a target in case of war. They and others feared that their very presence in British waters might involve the U.K., with no voice in the matter, in an American nuclear war. Understandably, Macmillan was in no hurry to reach agreement on the basing issue.[9]

But he signed the Skybolt agreement in September, fearful that any further delay would put the deal off until after the Presidential election in November, when a new Administration might not favor it. The U.S. also signed in September. It promised nothing but that we would do our best to develop Skybolt, and would sell it to the U.K. if we succeeded. Thereafter, the British continued to stall on berthing at Holy Loch. The U.S. threatened to go elsewhere in Europe. The British caved. On November 1, just days before the U.S. election, Macmillan publicly announced the berthing offer.[10] Watkinson noted that if the Americans ever had to abandon Skybolt, "they would have a moral obligation to help us to overcome, in one way or another, the difficulties this would cause for us." This theme, buried in classified British documents for decades, was to emerge as the fulcrum of the British political posture when the Skybolt crisis of 1962–63 erupted.

By the closing months of 1960, costs were mounting and so were project problems. News of DoD concerns about Skybolt reached the U.K. U.S. annual budget proposals were about to be released. Secretary Gates told Eisenhower that no new money was proposed for Skybolt, that moneys already appropriated would be stretched to cover the coming year, and that what might be *technically* achievable might cost too much to be considered *feasible*,[11] a term the British seemed to define as "not impossible." Gates warned the British that the administration could not irrevocably commit its successor to continuing the project. Macmillan was alarmed. Watkinson, equally concerned, noted that "the Prime minister had always viewed Skybolt as part of the bargain for the [Holy Loch] berthing facilities."[12] The British had moved quickly from trying to disassociate berthing as a quid-pro-quo for Skybolt to obliging the U.S. to come through on Skybolt or a suitable substitute, now that the U.S. had berthing rights on the Clyde.

CHANGING OF THE GUARD—1961–1962

In January 1961, John F. Kennedy became President; Robert McNamara became Secretary of Defense. At an early meeting with the President it was decided that the B-70 supersonic bomber, an iconic Air Force project, would be phased out. Herb York told me that the principals agreed that Skybolt would be used to "shoot down the B-70," meaning that Skybolt development would be allowed to continue until after the B-70 had been reduced to an R&D program with no production objectives, whereupon, after the political dust settled, it would be Skybolt's turn.[13]

The first Polaris tender arrived at Holy Loch in early 1961 amid a flurry of popular protests. Less than two years later, when the U.S. finally did inform the British that Skybolt was about to be cancelled, the Macmillan administration would claim that in canceling, the U.S. had broken its part of the "bargain:" we had Holy Loch; now they would have nothing; therefore we owed them something to preserve their Independent Nuclear Deterrent.

Meanwhile, Skybolt debates and press coverage grew in Parliament and the British press. The Loyal Opposition attacked Skybolt repeatedly. The name of the project was reified to conjure an actual missile long before even an experimental specimen had been built. It apparently no longer mattered much to British political leadership supporting Skybolt whether the weapon, if it were ever deployed, would work: Skybolt would deter so long as the Soviets thought it would, or that it might.[14] For almost two more years, Skybolt limped on as schedules lagged, costs rose, flight tests failed and development of the celestial-inertial guidance system dramatically lagged. The British posture stiffened as it aged.

PRELUDE TO CRISIS: AUGUST-SEPTEMBER 1962

But things had changed on the U.S. side. McNamara had radically altered the Pentagon management climate. "Program budgeting" required that every project be considered and reconsidered in context. Skybolt costs and test failures were mounting. Atlas, Titan and Polaris systems, the growing backbone of deterrence in the burgeoning Missile Age, had now been deployed.

Preparation of the 1963 Defense budget was well underway by the fall of 1962. On August 24, Charles Hitch, OSD Comptroller, and Harold Brown, Director of Defense Research and Engineering, discussed Skybolt at McNamara's request. All agreed that Skybolt was not really needed, that its development was highly speculative and that the growing budget overruns appeared to be out of control.[15]

But Skybolt was now a politically delicate matter. The prime contractor, Douglas Aircraft, had an influential Washington presence (and a London office, as well). The project remained a LeMay favorite, and he was now the Air Force Chief of Staff. Then there was the British question. "An Air Force general told a Budget Bureau aide in 1962: 'They can't cancel Skybolt on us. The British are with us. They won't do that to them.'"[16] So a leading question facing McNamara and Kennedy was: How can Skybolt be gracefully terminated in the face of the domestic opposition and British reactions that are likely to explode once the intention to do so becomes public? Hitch ingeniously proposed simply omitting Skybolt from the coming Defense budget proposal, so that when Congress debated the budget in 1963, Skybolt proponents on the Hill would have to argue for reinstating a huge program in the face of a large budget deficit and calls for tax cuts.[17]

But to prevent premature leaks, the time to cancel would have to be December, not before. McNamara agreed. He would face up to the British consequences when they had to be faced. Meanwhile, he would release production funds for Skybolt month-by-month, keeping the Air Force under scrutiny and lulling the British.

He revealed this to Brown and Hitch. Hitch told Alain Enthoven, his deputy, and Brown told me: cancellation later, silence now. The historian Richard Neustadt notes "Apparently no more was said by any of the four to anybody else for at least a month, and precious little until late October. Secrecy has rarely been as well maintained as by these men—and McNamara."[18]

THORNEYCROFT: SEPTEMBER-NOVEMBER 1962

The new Defence Minister, Peter Thorneycroft, accompanied by Solly Zuckerman, came to Washington in mid-September after these decisions had been taken. Thorneycroft had been Chancellor of the Exchequer, then Minister of Aviation, and would remain Minister of Defence until 1964. He had been seized with the conjoined issues of Skybolt and the British independent deterrent as part of the Macmillan government since before the Eisenhower-Macmillan Camp David accords. He was an Etonian, a member of the bar, and a very intelligent, experienced and exceptionally eloquent politician, diplomat and administrator.

He was given royal treatment. McNamara took him to SAC. The President invited him on a tour of several NASA space centers. When Skybolt came up, McNamara told Thorneycroft he was releasing some production funds but was concerned about rising costs and lagging schedules. Nothing was said about cancellation. Thorneycroft held forth on the Eisenhower-Macmillan understandings of 1960, which he knew well, recounting how the British understood it as an American commitment to help the U.K. maintain its independent nuclear deterrent. Maybe this last nuance was noted; maybe not. Thorneycroft returned to the U.K. "no wiser than he came."[19] Not until mid-October did Jerry Wiesner, the President's Science Advisor, or the Bureau of the Budget, know that Skybolt had been marked for termination. Even Paul Nitze, Assistant Secretary of Defense for International Security Affairs, was told only shortly before. [20]

I was in London on November 3 when Thorneycroft had me tracked down. He was at home, nursing a bad back. He asked me to come and see him. He had heard rumors. Was it true that Skybolt was to be cancelled? I said I had heard similar rumors, but that when I left Washington, there was nothing more. "Tell Bob," he said, "that we have depended upon you absolutely. Tell him it would be catastrophic if Skybolt were cancelled. Tell him the Government would fall."

I delivered this message to McNamara upon my return the next day. He said nothing. Thorneycroft, very uneasy, cabled McNamara on November 5, noting that the British press had reported the "first production order for Skybolt," and adding his hopes for Skybolt's success "which is, as you know, a central feature both of our defence policy and of our collaboration with you."

Thorneycroft's last sentence required that he be brought on board, and quickly. On November 7, four days after I met with Thorneycroft, McNamara and Nitze met with the President to discuss Skybolt. It was the eleventh day after the climactic end of the Cuba missile crisis. Chinese troops were on the march against India. Now there was the Thorneycroft business.

The question was: how to tell him what had not been officially, but had in fact been essentially decided, so that he would have time to think things over, but without leading the Air Force to think the decision had been made before the had spoken. On the same day, McNamara sent his draft defense budget to the Joint Chiefs of Staff. Skybolt was omitted from it for the coming year. First the Chiefs would have to respond. Then the President would decide. The Chiefs would make their position known on November 20.

McNamara told the President he would take care of informing the British. The American principals well knew that the British, having cancelled Blue Streak, relied entirely on Skybolt as their "independent deterrent." None, however, had the political investment in Skybolt that Macmillan had. He, but none of the others, had been there with Eisenhower in 1960. His fingerprints, not theirs, were on the project. He had a personal stake in the coming denouement and its resolution that none of the other actors had. For the Americans, ever-rising costs, formidable technical obstacles and the fundamental inutility of Skybolt even if it worked, drove the decision. For the British, an operational Skybolt, or at least the hope for it, was seen as the lynch-pin of the Conservative Party's political posture.

On November 8, McNamara saw the British Ambassador, David Ormsby Gore, informing him that while there was not yet a decision, Skybolt was being re-evaluated. Costs were rising. Its worth was in question. London ought to know. On the 9th Thorneycroft called McNamara, who repeated the story he had disclosed to Gore, and said he would be willing to come to London to discuss the matter. He estimated that the U.S. decision would not likely be made before December 10. The earliest London discussions would probably not be advisable before November 23.[21]

DECISION AND INDECISION—LATE NOVEMBER 1962

On November 20 the Chiefs, as was to be expected, recommended continuing Skybolt development. The Chairman, General Maxwell

Taylor, not subject to their collegial constraints, disagreed. The President approved cancellation, "subject to consultation with the British on alternatives. The Secretary of Defense had a decision; now he had to consult."[22]

Many alternatives for the British after Skybolt were discussed in State and Defense. Some disliked the British independent deterrent in any form. It encouraged France to imitate Britain's example. After France the Germans could be next. That could lead to a severe Soviet reaction. Many favored a multilateral force—in some of its embodiments, a mixed-crew multi*national* force—under NATO control. A few wished to see nothing that would strengthen the U.S./U.K. relationship to the detriment of multilateral diplomatic relations. Even mentioning providing the British with Polaris submarine-launched missiles as a substitute for Skybolt could evoke a chorus of dismay at State.

The British, too, pondered what was to be done when Skybolt was cancelled. Thorneycroft was caught in a dilemma. If SAC lost Skybolt, the U.K. would not want it, but he could not ask for Polaris instead. For one thing, he might be refused. Moreover, he could not afford to be seen as an advocate for Polaris as preferable to Skybolt in the eyes of his own Air Force, Navy, the aviation industry, or Prime minister Macmillan. He could accept, but could not advocate any substitute for Skybolt.

Thorneycroft had no interest in Hound Dog as a substitute. Its name alone struck unwanted resonances in Britain. Besides, Soviet air defenses would probably be increasingly effective against cruise missiles, while Polaris missiles launched from submarines, for which no defenses were in sight, would be far more credible. What was to be done? Macmillan hoped to bring the British into the European Common Market (EEC). For another, he wanted to keep the independent nuclear deterrent. He also wanted to maintain the "special relationship" between the U.K. and the U.S. The last thing he wanted was to have these objectives, mutually inharmonious in several ways, become the subject of choices exposed on the table of major negotiations. The British leadership analyzed many possible alternatives among themselves, but awaited the December meeting to discuss matters face-to-face.

McNamara, whatever his object, sent mixed signals to both the Air Force and the British. He spoke about cost-effectiveness, but he released production funds. More importantly, the Eisenhower-Macmillan agreement implied that the U.S. might have to cancel because of technical infeasibility, but said nothing about cost-effectiveness. If, however, the U.S. was going to cancel Skybolt because of "cost-effectiveness," the British, for whom cost, at least forensically, had nothing to do with "feasibility," would claim that we had a "moral obligation" to provide a suitable substitute for Skybolt.

British silence after the McNamara warning caused little anxiety in Washington. Some felt that silence suggested assent. Others were a little anxious when they thought about it, which was not much or often—everybody was busy. On December 10, armed with a comprehensive *aide memoire* prepared by delegates from State, the White House and Paul Nitze's OSD office of International Security Affairs, McNamara, Nitze and I took off for the London meeting with Thorneycroft.[23]

THE LONDON MEETING, DECEMBER 11, 1962

We landed at Gatskill, a minor airport compared with Heathrow. I was surprised to see a crowd of reporters huddled near the tarmac awaiting us. McNamara made a brief statement, noting that Skybolt would be discussed at the meeting with Thorneycroft scheduled for the afternoon, adding that the project was very costly and complex and that five flight tests had failed. Thorneycroft was there. Harold Watkinson, his predecessor, and other British officials, thought

McNamara's statements were egregiously inappropriate, tantamount to presupposing a dire outcome of talks yet to be held. Thorneycroft stayed calm. His turn would come in the afternoon.

Newspapers being hawked as we walked to our cars blared banner headlines screaming SKYBOLT DOUBLECROSS. What had fueled such a press eruption? Much later I learned that less than a week before, Hitch, for reasons tied to the budget process, told the military departments that Skybolt was to be terminated, warning as he did so that no disclosures were to be made. Leaks started at once. Articles appeared in the *New York Times* and the *Washington Post*. They were picked up in London. McNamara had figured that December 10 was the earliest leak date. He was off by about three days.

Our little group went to lunch. One historian reports that I recalled McNamara commenting that

> I've got a card up my sleeve but I'm going to let them play it; we give them Polaris on the understanding that they assign their subs to NATO. I think that's where we're going to come out. I'll start with my three options, then I think they'll ask for this.[24]

We drove to Whitehall and assembled in a small conference room around a simple library table. Thorneycroft sat at the head, with McNamara, Paul Nitze, David Bruce, our ambassador to London, and me on his left. Solly, joined by a couple of British staff, sat across from us. I took notes as verbatim and as inconspicuously as I could on a small pad of paper on my knee beneath the table. Thorneycroft led off with a peroration about the dreadful consequences of a Skybolt cancellation. McNamara took advantage of a pause to suggest that he read the *aide memoire* he had brought. Thorneycroft agreed. The document was about twenty pages long. It took about an hour to read it aloud. It recounted Skybolt's development history, its financial and technical difficulties leading to the decision to cancel it, and put forth some alternatives for the British to consider as a replacement for it. These included continuing the project at British expense; substituting Hound Dog; or joining a multinational force including many other European powers.

McNamara was under no illusion that the British would find any of these acceptable. He advanced them, however, to accord with instructions composed by the State Department. He favored Polaris as the solution, but awaited a British request for it. Thorneycroft favored it, too, but awaited an American offer.

THORNEYCROFT'S REPLY

Thorneycroft responded when McNamara finished. He began in a tone of grave earnestness, saying much what he had said to me a month before in his London home: "We depended upon you absolutely." He repeated this several times and, as I wrote, "He said it in a way that evoked images of the direst betrayal. I remember reflecting on his skill in evoking a sense of guilt, of obligation on the part of the Americans who had, in fact, done nothing more than cancel a development that should never have been started, to which the British had contributed nothing, for which the Americans had no real military need, and which the British had identified as their independent nuclear deterrent."[25]

His demeanor, his eloquence, his lawyerly skills were, for me, a simply brilliant display of diplomatic stagecraft. He made it appear, moreover, that he was almost surprised by all this, that his remarks were entirely unrehearsed, a spontaneous, heartfelt response to an unexpected confrontation, although he had known about the likelihood of the decision to cancel for more than a month. Here are some of Thorneycroft's words as I recorded them, excerpted from a published extract from my notes:[26]

I won't comment on the technical judgments. . . I am confident that your experts have advised you as you have indicated in your paper. I am equally confident that other experts could be found to argue the other side.

I will discuss the political implications. This missile is at the heart of British defence policy. It is the key to the continuing of the V-bomber force. It is the only example of complementarity between the U.S. and Great Britain.

Moreover, the Skybolt project arose as part of the context and complex of other decisions. We made the U.K. a target by agreeing to base Polaris at Holy Loch. That agreement and the Skybolt agreement were both taken in the same context.

He turned to the "grievous political consequences to me and my party."

We, on our side, of course, always said you would never let us down. We had to say that because we put our reliance in you absolutely. Now they will be able to say that they were right and we were wrong. . . .

He pointed to "recent statements" by American spokesmen, including McNamara, who raised questions in public speeches about problems attached to the British independent deterrent.

The British press, and many others will say the Skybolt decision is part of that policy. They will say this decision is really taken to force Britain out of having an independent nuclear deterrent.

. . . And so, Bob, I would like to ask you a question.

If you are going to cancel the project, are you going to say that it won't work, or are you going to say it will cost too much?

Here Thorneycroft was raising a question posed by the wording of the U.S.-U.K. agreements about Skybolt: they say nothing about cancelling for reasons of cost. McNamara said that "We won't say that it is impossible, but we will say that technical problems dominate the decision." Thorneycroft responded,

Of course, but most missiles slip their schedules. Most of these projects cost more. . . . Many of them are less accurate than they might be desired to be. But to cancel this project tears the heart out of our relations. . . .

A series of thrusts and parries ensued. McNamara asked if the British would continue the project alone if we cancelled it. Thorneycroft instantly snapped that this was the only interesting alternative. As historical research reveals, the British had already concluded that to continue the project with funding from London would be totally impractical. Thorneycroft brought up Polaris. Why hadn't McNamara mentioned that?

POLARIS

McNamara asked him if they would buy Polaris if we made it available. After some discussion, Thorneycroft asked why furnishing Polaris seemed to be such a problem for the Americans. McNamara said something about legal problems involving nuclear parts of the submarine. Solly offered an unrelated comment: if the U.S. dropped Skybolt for technical reasons, the U.K. shouldn't pick it up. McNamara responded that we kept it up only because of British interest in it. "You, Solly, have always known this. Your other experts have always known it, too." But Thorneycroft stayed on message.

> No, the question goes beyond Skybolt or the problems of Skybolt. We had Skybolt and you had the Polaris berthing at Holy Loch. You must go out of the decision on Skybolt, if you do, with another decision that is taken at the same time.

And that "other decision" must be to publicly support the British independent deterrent.

Nitze asked Thorneycroft "if they had considered the effect upon their relations to the Common Market" if the U.K. acquired Polaris as an independent force. Thorneycroft responded that that was their worry, and besides, de Gaulle "would have no legitimate grounds for complaint." [27] McNamara asked if the British would consider saying that Polaris would be part of a multilateral force. Thorneycroft responded firmly:

> Not as a condition upon us. After the announcement and the decision, then the U.K. can go into multilateral arrangements just as the U.S. can. But the U.K. must enter any such arrangement as an independent power.

At this point my recollection differs from the account given by Zuckerman in his autobiography. Solly writes that

> The concentration on the political repercussions of the cancellation was so intense, and the atmosphere was so charged, that I have completely forgotten exactly how the meeting ended, or what we did when we got up from the table. [28]

But I remember quite clearly. Thorneycroft ended the meeting saying "Let's all of us go home and have a bath. Let's have a bath." McNamara left to meet some friends. The remaining Americans retired to the American embassy. David Bruce borrowed my notes and sent a message to President Kennedy. A couple of hours later, on the way to our hotel, headlines proclaimed SKYBOLT CANCELLED. I thought the British had leaked. So, when he saw the headlines, did McNamara.

Solly—this, too, he wrote, he did not remember—and I had been charged with getting him set up to come to the States and begin coordination needed for the transfer of Polaris systems to the U.K. (Solly later wrote that a correspondent of the *Sunday Times* published a story recounting what followed that fully accords with my recollection.)

We were unable to meet after the conference. I had to leave for Washington the next day. Solly climbed into the back of a London cab with me as we drove off for Heathrow Airport early in the morning. We had the driver raise the soundproof glass partition that isolated him from the occupants, while we hurriedly discussed a long list of topics related to his charge. He left me at Heathrow.

Nothing came of that. The Polaris issue could not have been resolved by McNamara and Thorneycroft, although that was the ultimate outcome that McNamara expected and that Thorneycroft really sought, but which Kennedy and Macmillan would have to decide. They had been scheduled for several weeks to meet for a much-publicized summit at Eleuthra, a posh Nassau resort in the Bahamas, only eight days later. Now, unexpectedly, the summit spotlight would be on the Skybolt confrontation and its multiple political ramifications.

McNAMARA

McNamara returned to Washington a couple of days after me, and began preparing for the Nassau summit meeting. He called me to his office. He was standing behind his large desk. As he spoke he punched the edge of a sheet of paper with a three-hole punch, affixed little life-saver reinforcements to each hole, and inserted the page into the open rings of a large loose-leaf binder. He asked me for some papers I might have about Skybolt as he wrote the alphabetical tab index letter and the identity of the sheet just filed on the table-of-contents page for that bulky volume.

As I left I asked his aide if he had accumulated the materials that had already filled several large binders. General Brown said no, and added that he had no idea what was going on. "He does it all himself. He's been phoning all over the Pentagon all morning." It was also a lasting and valuable lesson. I organized my own files that way, starting that very day.

McNamara had dozens of such large loose-leaf files on a multitude of subjects which he compiled himself, all the while dealing with the monumental demands of his high office. He came to Congressional committee meetings armed with an array of such books. Members would sometimes test McNamara by asking how much money was in the DoD budget for some obscure little project. "Congressman, I don't recall exactly," he would say, reaching for one of the huge books arrayed around him. "But I believe it is about $51 million in the coming fiscal year." He would look it up as he was speaking and then quickly correct himself. "No, Congressman, it is actually $51.4 million."

I recall one episode among many that illustrates his capacity to focus and recall. McNamara asked me to come to his office with a paper I had prepared at his request dealing with Air Force bombers. He read the paper, delivered in a three-ring loose-leaf binder, as I sat in front of his desk. He was a speed reader. Every ten seconds or so he would flip a page with a decisive gesture that ended with an audible thump as his hand struck the desk top.

In moments he closed the book, having read several thousand words. "On page three, paragraph two, you say…. Why is that true?" I quickly turned to the page he had indicated, trying to recall the context. I had a sinking feeling that McNamara knew what I had written better than I did.

Certainly McNamara was a very smart man, like many men who ascend to high places on their merits. In addition, he had exceptional self-discipline. He read voraciously, undaunted by the volumes of diverse information he had to absorb, much of it information he solicited. One of his first acts upon taking office was to request White Papers dealing with a multitude of issues. His special assistant at the time, Cyrus Vance, asked me to suggest the format for white papers, possibly because I had sent some to McNamara's predecessor, Tom Gates. It was adopted by McNamara with little change. First on the list of papers, soon referred to as the "96 Trombones" (from a popular tune of the day, *76 Trombones,* from the musical "The Music Man.") was to be a comprehensive statement of national strategic policy; a task near the end of the list called for the analysis of some comparatively minor weapon development. Many White Papers bulked up to tens of single-spaced pages. Just the first responding documents must have totaled about 500,000 words. Many included critical technical details.

I was responsible for preparing several of these White Papers. One of the first dealt with an Air Force project for a nuclear-powered plane that McNamara eventually cancelled. Our first try came back within the hour it was sent to McNamara, marked up with a multitude of marginal notes and questions. We tried again, with the same result. I asked him what we were doing wrong. "Nothing," he said. "Just make it comprehensive and complete. Don't try to oversimplify or summarize or to keep it short. Just make it comprehensive and complete."

His example motivated his staff. He arrived at his office at about 7:30 AM and left about twelve hours later. One day he lectured a meeting of several of his key people, referring to one of the Assistant Secretaries who was working very long hours and was showing the strain. "I told Tom," he said, "that I don't want to see people working long hours. It just wears you out. I told Tom," he added in all seriousness, "'I don't want to see you in this building one minute after 7:30 at night.'"

As many have noted, even the best and the brightest have limitations. Like the tallest tree, they tend to attract the most lightning. McNamara was no exception; but I never saw his equal in focus, concentration, retention, grasp and drive. I remember him with great admiration and deep respect.

NASSAU

The Skybolt crisis filled the British papers in the aftermath of the McNamara-Thorneycroft conference. The *Washington Post* took up the cry in an editorial accusing the administration of diplomatic incompetence, of failing to honor the Eisenhower-Macmillan agreement, and of unconcern for British needs and feelings. Fears and suspicions had grown on both sides. Thorneycroft suspected that the Americans were bent on ending the British independent nuclear deterrent by cancelling Skybolt. American advisors feared selling Polaris to the U.K. would spread independent nuclear forces to France and even Germany. Thorneycroft had reflected the British position when he told McNamara that if the U.S. cancelled Skybolt, the U.S. would be obliged to publicly support the U.K.'s independent deterrent, and reiterated that Polaris, were it offered as a substitute for Skybolt, must come with no strings attached. Kennedy and his advisors wanted NATO strings to avoid threatening the unity of European nuclear policy. If events had made Thorneycroft deeply suspicious of American motives, the Americans had not fully gauged the passions that linked Skybolt to Britain's insistence on an independent nuclear deterrent, or the centrality of this issue to the Tory Party's political posture.

The Americans had no further interest in Skybolt. Whatever dim British hopes remained for it vanished quickly at Nassau. Solly and I and most of McNamara's notebooks were not needed, with the exception of one memorable moment, when, late in the afternoon of the second day, McNamara strode into the hotel lobby where I was standing. He told me to secure a copy of the Eisenhower-Macmillan Agreement of 1960, and get it to him by 7 AM the following morning. "Seven o'clock." he said. "Not a minute later." The British had no need of a copy. Macmillan had been a party to it. Thorneycroft, too, could probably have recited it from memory. But the Camp David agreement had marked a turning point. It made Skybolt the centerpiece of an international compact, irrevocably bound to the fevered issue of the U.K. independent deterrent.

That was about two years after the U.S. and U.K. Air Forces had begun to cook up the project in the first place. Then, 1958, (with the unmemorable title: the ALBM—Air Launched Ballistic Missile), it had been far below the American policy radar, and remained there even when it was reborn as Skybolt in January 1960. Its political gestation was solemnized by the Camp David Agreement in March 1960. With Nassau, it became an international *cause celebre*. Now Kennedy was at the U.S. helm; Macmillan still led the U.K.; back home, Eisenhower, a Republican hero, was still alive and well in Pennsylvania; General de Gaulle loomed in Paris.

Solly joined me in my room. Room service brought us dinner. The White House operator quickly found the home phone number of Admiral Martell, a Navy assignee to our office. I gave him the combination to my office safe and described the folder where he would find the document. He called me from the Pentagon and dictated the short memo over the phone. The paper was probably stamped "SECRET," but there was no choice except to use the open line. By 7AM McNamara had his copy, the key critical document missing from his voluminous files. Except for that, I was not needed. Nor was Solly. Neither General LeMay nor any U.S. military figures had been invited. Skybolt had long since become a political, not a military, matter. Nassau was a diplomatic, not a technical summit.

STRAINS, CONSEQUENCES, QUESTIONS

However, unlike the Americans, the British, who seem to have clung to a last ember of hope that Skybolt could be resuscitated, brought a contingent of technical specialists. I discovered that on the first day, Thorneycroft addressed these aides,

> saying that he recognized two schools of thought on Skybolt; the view of a powerful minority body of experts who were against it, and the views of a large body of practical and responsible people on both sides of the Atlantic who were close to the project and who maintained that it was technically feasible and sensible. He gave full weight to the latter . . . and therefore he would not subscribe to any joint statement which agreed to cancel Skybolt because it was technically unsound."[29]

One of the aides spoke at length with me later that day, and concluded that "the DoD damning of Skybolt on technical grounds was a trumped-up affair," adding that "In retrospect, I was horrified at the thought that the workings of the largest Democracy in the West could in any way be influenced by someone so shallow as Rubel" whom he identified as "long an under-cover opponent of Skybolt."[30]

Solly later recounted how a former Chief of the Air Staff wrote to *The Times*, hinting that cancellation was all part of a plot. Another retired Air Marshall opined that "It is a really appalling thought that a couple of Ministers and a zoologist [i.e.: Solly Zuckerman] can slip off to the Bahamas and, without a single member of the Chiefs of Staff Committee present, commit us to a military monstrosity [i.e. Polaris] on the purely political issue of nuclear independence."[31]

The paranoia, anger and resentments that boiled beneath top British levels remained concealed beneath Macmillan's and Thorneycroft's veneer of diplomatic demeanor and passionate rhetoric. I never imagined the force of subterranean perceptions and emotions that long-classified documents only recently revealed.[32] Nothing is clearer, however, than that nobody involved in the Skybolt controversy had the panoramic view of it briefly sketched here, nearly a half-century later, as long-buried documents bob to the surface.

Macmillan came closest to understanding most of the story. By early 1960 he already knew enough about this American development to cross the Atlantic to secure it for Great Britain at a time when it is doubtful that even the Secretary of Defense, not to mention the President, knew much about the project. Even then his first choice would have been Polaris, which he knew was off the table. At the time, and for the next two-and-a-half years, both bomber forces fiercely supported Skybolt. The USAF hoped that involving the British would virtually guarantee support for a favorite LeMay project. Nassau dashed all that on both sides of the Atlantic. In the end, however, Britain got Polaris submarines and missiles without warheads, ambiguously assigned to NATO, but which could, at the Queen's discretion, revert to exclusive British control as an "independent deterrent." It was more than Macmillan had expected.

A month later, seizing upon this bilateral deal as an example of Britain's non-European character and its special trans-Atlantic relationships, General de Gaulle denied Great Britain entry into the European Common Market. Back in America, Skybolt disappeared from the budget and faded from headlines. The Air Force said little or nothing. Both the U.S. and, after us, the British, looked for something salvageable when the project was definitively stopped soon after Nassau, but found nothing. Skybolt had cost nearly $2.6 billion in 1996 dollars.

Near the end of the Nassau summit I was summoned to a meeting where President Kennedy presided. Sitting in his rocking chair, talking to McGeorge Bundy, he mused about the momentous negotiations that had erupted so quickly and would reverberate on the international stage for years to come. Puzzled, he asked: "Who is the wooer and who is the wooed?"

PARTIAL BIBLIOGRAPHY

Aldous, Richard. *Macmillan Eisenhower and the Cold War*. Four Courts Press, Ltd, Dublin 8, Ireland, 2005.

Brookings Institution. U.S. Nuclear Weapons Cost Study Project. Skybolt Air-Launched Ballistic Missile *(GAM-48-A.)* In re Skybolt development costs. www.brookings.edu/projects/archive/nucweapons/skybolt.aspx

"Cabinets and the Bomb Workshop (Session Two)". *The British Academy Review*. www.britac.ac.uk/pubs/review/perspectives/0703cabinetsandbomb-2.html

Illuminating reminiscences by a *grou*p of more than twenty former defence officials and staff recalling Skybolt, Nassau and other matters decades past.

DeGaulle's Veto on British membership of the EEC. His speech of 14 January 1963 in full. http://en.wikisource.org/wiki/SeGaulle's_Veto_on_British_membership_or_the_EEC

Kaplan, Lawrence S.; Landa, Ronald D.; Drea, Edward J. *The McNamara Ascendancy 1961-1965*. Historical Office of the Secretary of Defense, Superintendent of Documents, U.S. Government Printing Office, 2006.

A uniquely comprehensive, authoritative and well-written account of a revolutionary period in U.S. Defense Department history.

Landa, Ronald D. "The Origins of the Skybolt Controversy in the Eisenhower Administration" in *Seeing Off the Bear: Anglo-American Air Power Cooperation During the Cold War*, edited by Roger G. Miller, 117-31. Washington, D.C.: Air Force History and Museums Program, 1995.

This excellent paper includes many detailed references to original American and British internal documents from the Skybolt period, including several of my own.

Neustadt, Richard E. *Report to JFK: The Skybolt Crisis in Perspective*. Ithaca: Cornell University Press, 1999.

President Kennedy, taken aback by the emergence of the Skybolt controversy late in 1962, commissioned the historian Richard Neustadt to determine how it arose and what, at bottom, it was all about. Neustadt's study begins in the fall of 1962. However, apart from background information and an account of the Eisenhower-Macmillan agreement of early 1960, nothing about the roots of Skybolt dating to before 1958-59 appears in this account. He observes that I was the only U.S. official involved with the project from its inception to its cancellation; today, only McNamara among the chief actors is still alive. As I have noted, the who, what, why where and when of the Air Force-RAF collaboration that initiated the program has never been detailed. Kennedy's question at Nassau remains unanswered: Who is the wooer and who is the wooed?

Zuckerman Archives, www.archiveshub.ac.uk/news/<u>zuckerman.html</u>

Zuckerman, Lord Solly. Monkeys, Men and Missiles. An Autobiography, 1946-88. Collins, London 1988

The author devotes a long chapter to the Skybolt episode, drawn from his own records and a similar piece I sent him at his request. His account adds interestingly to mine.

7

TENSING NORGAY

When Tenzing Norgay and Edmund Hillary became the first to reach the top of Mt. Everest on May 29, 1953, few had ever heard their names. By the time they had descended 12,000 feet to Base Camp at almost 18,000 feet, they were world-famous. It had been forty-four years since men first reached the North Pole and forty-two since they reached the South Pole across the forbidding reaches of Antarctica. No one had even set out to conquer Mt. Everest until the British expedition of 1921. All told, some fourteen expeditions set out on Everest over the thirty-two years prior to 1953. Fifteen men died. Eleven expeditions attempted and failed to reach the summit At last, in 1953, three-quarters of a century after men had reached the first two poles, Tenzing and Hillary reached the far more remote and hostile "third pole," Everest's summit. Only sixteen years later Neil Armstrong and Buzz Aldrin would walk on the moon. Yuchiro Miura skied down Everest one year after that.

Now hundreds join private expeditions up Everest every year. Some 200 frozen corpses lie somewhere along the way. More than 1,400 individuals have reached the top. The most feasible paths to the summit are now well known. Every item of clothing and equipment has been markedly improved by experience and burgeoning technology. High-altitude physiology has been exhaustively studied.

But thin air, dangerous terrain and terrible storms have not changed. Everest still claims many victims among those following the Hillary-Tensing route, and among daring climbers trying more dangerous and difficult approaches. Statistics from nearly sixty expeditions indicate that the chance of putting at least one member on the top is about the same as the chance that the group will experience at least one fatality on the way up or down. Tenzing's and Hillary's calculable chances were far worse. Theirs was the fifteenth expedition and the twelfth to try for the summit. Bourdillon and Evans had been turned back just 300 feet from the summit utterly exhausted only three days before Hillary and Tenzing made the successful second attempt. The scoreboard when they set out was fifteen expeditions, fifteen fatalities, twelve tries for the summit, zero successes.

In mid-December 1978 Robin and I joined an Australian group for a month-long trek along the trail leading from the small airfield at Lukla (9,000 feet) to the Everest Base Camp at Kala Pattar (about 18,000 feet). Tenzing himself was to be our honorary leader. The paying trekkers were ten Australians and four Americans. Our actual leader was Philip Temple, a charming and accomplished New Zealander. A small plane took us to Lukla on the short flight from Kathmandu. There we met Tenzing for the first time.

Lukla was little more than a short, grassy airstrip in the midst of a forested area. It was bounded at the approach end by a perpendicular drop of thousands of feet, and the other end by a vertical cliff thousands of feet high. Landing errors had led to a heap of plane wreckage at the bottom of the valley, and some next to the airstrip. A couple of small buildings and a wind-sock were the only cultural features to be seen. Our sirdar, Nima Tsering, and the Sherpa and Sherpani porters in his charge, were already there. Our plane brought in the last of the trekkers and their baggage. Each porter would carry up to 30 pounds of a trekker's personal necessities, stuffed into a duffel bag. Expedition food, tents and other supplies were likewise suspended on the porter's back by a taup line around the forehead. We carried only an extra sweater and a few odds and ends in a light back-pack. All told there were about forty-five in our little expedition.

As porters sorted out hundreds of pounds of baggage alongside the runway, two little kids, a boy and a girl, each about seven, drifted over to watch the excitement. Each stood with rocks they had been gathering from the airstrip in half-filled bags hanging from the customary taup line around the forehead. The emptied airplane roared off for Kathmandu in a cloud of dust. Dust and a relative silence fell. We trekkers, colorful in bright jackets fresh from far-distant lands sat on the ground waiting for the leader's signal to start. Porters sat by their assigned loads. The sirdar bustled among them. Motionless, the two children, seemingly untroubled by their heavy bags of rocks, stared at us. Equally dumb-stuck, we stared back.

We were soon on the trail northward toward the busy market town of Namché Bazar. Along the way, Tenzing told us tales about the 1953 Everest expedition which had followed this same route. The entire route from Lukla to Base Camp below Kala Pattar has since been named the "Hillary/Tenzing Trail." He sketched the expedition's staggering statistics.

There were no planes from Kathmandu to Lukla in 1953. The entire Everest expedition trekked 175 miles from Kathmandu to Base Camp. There were no roads. Everything moved on trails, rising from south to north, rising and descending east-west across endless drainages carved by melting snows from the Himalayan peaks.

The expedition of more than 400 people employed more than 350 porters. It carried 7.5 tons of equipment and supplies "contained in 443 packages, each numbered and listed down to the last matchbox." Thirty porters were required to carry the cash to be paid to the Sherpas as they earned their pay week by week. There were dozens more in the expedition crew. Of these, eleven were climbers, including Tenzing, a historic first for a Sherpa.[1] Hillary had been on Everest once before. Tenzing, by then the most experienced Everest climber in the world, had been there six times, beginning as a porter in 1935, and climbing above 28,000 feet with the Swiss in 1952.

An influx of tourists that started as a trickle when the country was first opened to outsiders in 1951 grew to a flood after Everest was conquered in 1953. Nepal became the favored gateway to Everest and a boulevard for thousands of sightseeing trekkers tramping through remote highland villages in growing numbers every year. Now, as we passed through twenty-five years later, once-dense pine forests had largely disappeared, but the endless panoramas of Himalayan peaks streaming banners of wind-blown snow, and spreading landscapes of terraced hillsides below them built up stone by stone for centuries, remained only slowly mutable beneath the winds and snows of time.

In 1953, many Nepalese living in the highlands had never before seen a European, a wrist watch, or anything like the paraphernalia of a major expedition. Ever since, multiple expeditions and thousands of trekkers and other tourists have led to an explosion of population and felt needs while eroding local languages and cultures, leaving the country relatively more resource-poor than ever before. Nepal's population figures highlight the story. From the time Tenzing was born in 1914 until he left Nepal for India in the early 1930s, population remained essentially unchanged at about 5.5 million. By 1978-79 when we met him, population was nearly three times greater, about 14 million. In 2008, it had doubled to more than 27 million, still growing at the alarming rate of 2.7% per year. If sustained, Nepal's population will double again in just over 25 years. Between 1991 and 2001 the Kathmandu valley added a million inhabitants, 2.5 times its 1991 level. The traditional terraced farms and grazing herds can no longer sustain the indigenous population nor be maintained by a shrinking rural workforce.

Nepal remains distant, but no longer isolated. One day a small boy about ten years old joined me as we passed through a highland village. Striding next to me for minutes on the trail, speaking good English, he said: "Give me your jacket."

I told him I couldn't do that. He asked why not?

"Because we are going to much higher places where it is cold, and I will need my jacket."

"Yes," he said, "but you are rich. I am poor."

Tenzing was a product of the old Nepal. The foreign forces that transformed Nepal blew in from every quarter of the sixteen-point winds during his lifetime. It was hard for us to realize that Tenzing, like the majority of Nepalese of his generation, was illiterate, or that a man of his urbanity had grown up in a remote village near Thamé long before Nepal allowed foreigners into the country.

Soon after international fame descended upon him, Tenzing selected an American, James Ramsey Ullman, to ghost-write his autobiography. *Tiger of the Snows* was published in 1955. In it he writes that on the earlier expeditions the British referred to the Sherpa porters as "coolies." They were paid a pittance. Those who were injured or died on an expedition received little or no compensation. Gradually, those who were willing and able to climb to high altitudes, often carrying 50 pounds, and sometimes more, gained some recognition. After the 1938 expedition led by the Briton H. W. Tilman, these "tigers" as they had come to be informally known were awarded an official Tiger Medal, a mark of rank entered into their record books. It was on Tilman's expedition that Tenzing, along with others who had ascended to Camp Six at 27,200 feet, received his medal. Tenzing wrote that:

> One interesting thing about this expedition was that it was the first time I saw oxygen equipment. Tilman did not like oxygen—he though Everest should, and could, be climbed without it—and most of the others did not use it, either. . . most of the Sherpas laughed and called it "English air."

Tenzing describes how

> We waited [at Camp Five] and made ready to go on farther and establish Camp Six, which would be the highest. But the two Sherpas behind us who were carrying tents and fuel up from the col² could not get to Camp Five; and this made trouble, because we could not go on without these things. . . The other Sherpas at Camp Five said that if they were sent down they wanted to stay down, but I said I would go down and get the things and come back again. So I went alone. I found the tents and fuel about halfway down to the col, where the two Sherpas had left them before turning around, and slinging them on my back, started back up.

He slipped on the ice. In those days they did not wear crampons, steel shoe-spikes. He barely avoided sliding a mile down the steep mountainside to the vast glacier below.

> Fortunately it was all right, though. I went on, and reached Camp Five just before dark, and Smythe and

Shipton congratulated me. Later, when the expedition was over, I was given a special reward of 20 rupees.[3]

It is interesting to compare this account from *Tiger of the Snows* with a transcription of Tensing's account recorded on our 1978-79 expedition, for which I am indebted to my good friend, Graeme Kelleher. He was one of the ten Australian trekkers. We hit it off during our weeks on the trail, and have been in frequent touch for the thirty years since.

So in 1952, the first expedition was the Swiss expedition. They arrive in Nepal. Kathmandu was very simple—no motor cars, no planes and nothing hotel—a very small, simple city. Everything had to be carried. The first day, the French brought one jeep, and we saw this 100 people getting off at Kathmandu. This was the first time we saw this.

Kathmandu airport was where we camped. We set off from there. We start with 1,500 porters. Kathmandu is at an altitude of 4,500 feet. Base Camp is at 19,000. [Elsewhere he says it is at 17,500]. It is a very long way.

We first visit the Khumbu glacier—it is very terrible. So many crevasses. We have not the aluminium ladder, we have not a rope ladder. We had a lot of trouble. We sent back from Base Camp to Thyangboché, to bring some wood to make a bridge. We carry 55 timbers. We make ten bridges. But the trouble is, ice is moving down every day, every hour, and damaging the bridges.

Anyway, that was a first experience for us. We had Raymond Lambert and myself, we had no food, no oxygen and we reached the first time 28,215 feet and in 24 hours we are dead.[4]

Tenzing summarized his life trajectory as "from a coolie, a bearer of loads, to a man with a row of medals on his coat," from the more than faintly pejorative "coolie" to the insignia of transient fame. In a parallel frame, Hillary is sometimes referred to as a New Zealand bee-keeper who climbed Everest. Both had exceptional capacities and drive formed in worlds not only thousands of miles, but cultural centuries apart, combined in partnership and ultimate victory. Hillary came from the global English-speaking world. Tenzing was a product of the Solo Khumbu hills and valleys, framed by awesome Himalayan peaks, speaking a language that has no written form, a world where there actually *is* a mountain pass called Changri La.

Tenzing earned his honors by a rare combination of physical and mental abilities. He was about 5 feet 8 inches tall, above average for Sherpa men, and weighed about 160 pounds, which he says was thinner than average. He often mentions his "third lung" to explain his unusual endurance at high altitudes, even compared with other Sherpas[5] who, on the whole, are genetically better adapted to high altitudes than Caucasians. He was also exceptionally intelligent and powerfully motivated. Unlike the many Sherpas for whom carrying loads was simply a way to earn money, Tenzing wanted to *climb*, not just to carry.

> Always to make journeys, to move, to go and see and learn, has been like a thing in my blood.

Early-on he spoke enough English to enhance his chances of being chosen for many expeditions. His French was more limited, but *Ça va bien*—it's okay—served him well with French and Swiss expeditions. By 1953, having gone on British expeditions and spent years in India among British people, he declared that:

Now my English is good enough so I could tell much of the story in this book without an interpreter. Also I have traveled with men of other nationalities and tongues and do not always have to be a dummy. French?—*Ça va bien, mes braves!*. German?—*Es geht gut!* Italian? *Molto bene!*

Everything was *not* okay as Tenzing and Hillary approached the summit. Ahead and above them lay the last few hundred feet to the top that had never been climbed. Bourdillon and Evans, the first team chosen, had been forced back only 300 feet from the summit two days before. Evans' oxygen equipment had malfunctioned.[6] He had to take six breaths every time he took one more step. Bourdillon feared he would lose his fingers if he removed his glove to try adjusting Evans' equipment. They turned back, apparitions coated in ice from head to toe, utterly exhausted.

Hillary wrote a succinct and vivid description of their last dash for the top. He describes the great, menacing slopes below, the difficulty breathing, how the South Summit loomed overhead when they reached 28,000 feet, his anxious search for a route to the top. Four hundred feet from the summit they faced formidable steeps. Loose rock and snow in one direction looked dangerous. A snow-field lay ahead. Its weak crust gave way beneath their feet. They plowed through, buried in snow up to the hips. Exhausted, Hillary paused to gaze down between his legs to a void 10,000 feet below:

> "What do you think of it, Tenzing?" And the immediate response: "Very bad, very dangerous." "Do you think we should go on?" and there came the familiar reply that never helped you much but never let you down: "Just as you wish."

On the summit, Hillary's thoughts turned to the heroic attempts by former expeditions, of Mallory and Irvine who had lost their lives on the mountain thirty years before.

> Meanwhile, Tenzing had also been busy. On the summit he'd scratched out a little hole in the snow, and in this he placed some small offerings of food—some biscuits, a piece of chocolate, and a few sweets—a small gift to the Gods of Chomolungma which all devout Buddhists (as Tenzing is) believe inhabit the summit of this mountain. Besides the food, I placed the little cross that John Hunt [the Expedition leader] had given me on the South Col. Strange companions, no doubt, but symbolical at least of the spiritual strength and peace that all peoples have gained from the mountains.

They descended carefully. Tenzing carried several bags of equipment including a camera one of the British climbers had forgotten. "The sahibs," he writes, "left most of their things at Camp Eight (the highest, 27,900 feet)." At Camp Five the Sherpas insisted on carrying Tenzing's load the rest of the way down.

Here is Graeme Kelleher's transcription of Tenzing's account of the ascent to the summit:

> . . . Tent in rock and ice. That evening Hillary checking oxygen, Tenzing cooking tea, biscuits, salmon, chocolate. Decided to use new socks, put on boots and sleep dressed. Woke at 5:00 AM, had tea. Hillary did not wear boots [as he slept, and they were frozen when he awoke.] Cooked his boots on primus half hour— bad smell. Started 6:30 and carried three oxygen each (20 pounds each). Threw one each away at South Col.

When reached South Summit, saw what looked like summit, climbed it, then another, then another and at last, from west—see real summit. Reached at 11:30. Embraced, took many photos. Heavy wind. Stayed 15 minutes then start down. Always more tired on way down—dangerous—tendency to be careless. Very slowly, reached Noyce at South Col where they drank kerosene by mistake. Next morning, George Rowe came up from advance Base Camp and led them back. Hunt so excited his teeth fell out.

At Camp Four (21,200 feet) they met the main part of the expedition to great jubilation. As Hillary approached his team he declared: "Well George, we knocked the bastard off!" Tenzing recalls the evening there as the happiest in his life:

But, although I did not know it then, certain things had already begun to happen, which were later to cause much difficulty and misunderstanding.

The first of these was a false report that the expedition had failed. The correct information was wired to London, but was withheld for a day so that the news of this spectacular British achievement could become a special feature of the Queen's Coronation.

For the British the timing was perfect, and there was a wonderful celebration. But for many Easterners it was quite the opposite, for they did not receive the news until a day later—and then from the other side of the world. This was true even for King Tribhuvana of Nepal, in whose country Everest stands.

Tenzing sent a message to his wife that was not intended to be made public, and was not:

> "Myself along with one sahib reached summit Everest 29th May. Hope you will feel happy. Cannot write more. May I be excused." And at the bottom I myself signed my name.

Later there was "loose talk" that he had been paid by the British to delay releasing the news locally, and bribed to say that Everest had been climbed when in reality it had not been. Tenzing could not have imagined the tumult, pettiness and mendacity that would erupt around him after Everest. Nor had he given much thought to his future. Perhaps, after resting for a time in Darjeeling, he would build a new little house:

> It was not long, though, before I began to see that things were going to be very different from before. Already at Thyangboche [about 12,000 feet, the site of a large monastery] there was a wireless for me from Sir Winston Churchill . . . each day there were bigger crowds and more excitement.

They were soon surrounded by journalists hungry for interviews, including *Life* magazine, *The London Times* and the United Press Association. In the end, Tenzing signed a contract with UP. It was a canny move on his part, but one which deepened the divide between *Sherpa* and *Sahib* to which he often alludes:

> The English could not do anything like this. Before starting they had signed an agreement that all stories and photographs would belong to the expedition as a whole,

which in turn had its contract with the *Times*. But, though ranked as an expedition member, I had not been asked to do this, so that now I was free to deal with whom I chose. When we reached Kathmandu, and later New Delhi, there was some discussion and argument about this, for the *Times* thought that it had the rights to the story of *everyone* on the expedition; and Col. Hunt offered me 500 rupees a month for eight months if I would sign the agreement like the others. But I declined to do this. For the first time in my life I was in a position to make a considerable sum of money, and I could not see why it was not right and proper for me to do so.

These were only among the first of Tenzing's strange encounters of many kinds in the unfamiliar and often slippery world into which fame had cast him. He realized he was a lucky man. He realized, too, as he learned more about the greater world, that he was "an unlettered man" and that, at forty, it is not easy to acquire the knowledge and abilities that come with early education. He was dismayed by the hue and cry about whether he or Hillary first stepped on the very top, or whether he was Nepalese or Indian. Only months after Everest, recounting his lifelong search for adventure and love of being on the move, he writes:

> . . . as for all men, I suppose, there have been good and bad, rewards and problems, all mixed up together. Sometimes the crowds around me have been so thick, the pressures so great, that I have thought gloomily that a normal life is no longer possible; that my only chance for happiness is to go off with my family to some solitary place where we can live in peace.

By the end of 1978, the year we began our trek with Tenzing, there had been twenty-five more expeditions. Eighty-two more people, including three women, had made it to the top. Twenty-four more had died (including a fourth woman on her way down from the summit), just about one for every expedition. World-famous at thirty-nine, with a drawer full of medals, Tenzing was now sixty-four years old. Nearly half the people living in 1978 had been born too late to remember the conquest of Everest. Tenzing, for millions, had outlived his fame. Trekking with us he was a well-dressed, aging Sherpa, still the most famous Asian in the Far East, who carried himself with exceptional modesty and unflagging dignity. He ate with the Sherpas, not with us. He walked with us, not with them. In *Tenzing After Everest* (1977) he wrote about a trekking expedition like ours that he had accompanied for the first time a couple of years before:

> For the first time on an expedition I felt on equal terms with my employers; indeed I felt towards them not as Sherpa to Sahibs, but rather as friends.

Graeme Kelleher, reviewing this chapter, reports that Tenzing, however reserved, "certainly reacted with us as a friend. On Christmas Eve we shared a bottle of whiskey which I had brought for this occasion, We had a hilarious time in the hut with the other Sherpas and the Sherpanis. The next day, Tenzing said he had a bilious attack. I had a hangover."

Near the end of our journey our group sat around for a couple of days at Lukla waiting for a plane to Kathmandu; Tenzing, however, vanished without saying goodbye. Someone said he had an appointment with the King. Our sirdar, in a tone of deep disdain, rhetorically asked what *Tenzing* had to do with the King. "He's not Nepalese," he said. "He's Indian." A year before Tenzing had written:

Many people back in my homeland are dissatisfied with
me, the people of Solu Khumbu and even the King of
Nepal himself, because, they say, I left Nepal to live and
work in India and have done nothing for my own people.

A year or so before we met him he had lost his job as Director
of Field Training at the Himalayan Mountaineering Institute in
Darjeeling after more than twenty years there. Nehru himself had
assured him at the start that he would have his job and pay for life,
the easy assurance of a master politician now dead nearly fifteen
years. Tenzing was left with neither job nor retirement benefits. He
had never had a contract. He said he had never had a raise.

With a poignant mingling of naiveté and dismay, the plaint of a
herder boy whose fame and fortunes have faded with age and time,
he also writes that

. . . however much the rest of the world has accepted me
for what I am, in India I have always been out of the show.
And I do not really know why.

In India he was "Tenzing Sherpa." In Nepal, he was an ex-pat
who no longer belonged in the land of his birth. Abroad, he was
a stranger in strange lands. At home in Darjeeling he was saddled
for decades with people claiming to be related, demanding and
ungratefully accepting his largesse. Among us his occasional talks
were mostly about Everest, but little or nothing about his many great
adventures before that, and little about his heroic acts on the 1953
expedition, which included saving Hillary's life. Perhaps his reserve
screened—or betrayed—a certain weariness.

One day I found myself walking with Tenzing on the trail back
down to Kunde. He often walked alone, or with the sirdar's five-

year-old son, his frequent companion. I have a picture of the two of them walking toward me, the indefatigable little boy holding one end of Tenzing's ice-axe, Tenzing holding the other, the little Sherpa connected through that axe to the greatest Sherpa of them all.

Tenzing, the little boy, and I were alone. The trail approached a meadow that flourished in a modest depression the size of a football field. Near the middle of this field stood a small stone hut, fashioned from granite bricks tailored by hand. Behind it towered the great snow-capped Himalayan peaks rising some 15,000 feet above where we stood at about 12,000. Patches of green forest and terraced rice fields crowned with tattered prayer flags fluttering perpetual prayers to the somewhere-seeing gods stretched far away south and west. We stopped at the edge of the field. "You see that stone hut over there?" he asked.

I did.

He explained that he had been living in that hut tending his father's herd of yaks, when he decided to leave Nepal and go to India, specifically, to Darjeeling. He was sixteen, he said.

"What did you do?" I asked.

Tenzing said he just got up and started walking. He told no-one he was leaving or where he was going. He walked to Darjeeling where he joined a colony of Sherpas who served as expedition porters. Darjeeling was Tenzing's home for the next forty-five years.[7]

Tenzing volunteered another bit of information as we stood on the trail gazing at the hut he left so many years before. "You know," he said, "my name was not Tenzing Norgay when I was born."

I had not known that.

"Yes," he said, "when I was about four years old they discovered that I was the reincarnation of a business man from a nearby village who had died a few years before. His name had been Tenzing Norgay, so they renamed me."[8]

I told him I found that very interesting, which I did, reflecting on the oddity that close to half the world would find it perfectly believable, and the rest, quaintly the opposite.

I asked him a question. "Tenzing," I said, "you have been all over the world. I saw and heard you speak in Los Angeles a couple of years ago. You have been to Paris, Berlin, London and many other European cities. You have seen and met people living in many different ways and places. Tell me: if you had a perfectly free choice, where would you live?"

"Antarctica," he said.

"Well, no, Tenzing," I said, "I don't mean a place where they would have to fly in your food and supplies. I mean a place where the ordinary needs of life are reasonably at hand."

"Yes," he said, "Antarctica. It's very quiet there."

PARTIAL BIBLIOGRAPHY

Alan Arnette, Mt. Everest South Col Route
www.alanarnette.com/alan/everestsouthroutes.php

A photographic depiction of the South Col route, illustrated and described in useful detail.

Mount Everest, Wikipedia
http://en.wikipedia.org/wiki/Mount_Everest

Eighteen pages, illustrated, interesting histories.

Tenzing Norgay & James Ramsey Ullman, Tiger of the Snows, The autobiography of TENZING OF EVEREST, Bantam Books, New York 1955 (Bantam edition 1956)

"Norgay" is not Tenzing's last name. Tenzing Norgay, like Sherpa Tenzing or Tenzing Sherpa, is one of his designations. This volume was composed during the year after Everest.

Tenzing Norgay & Malcom Barnes, Tenzing After Everest, An autobiography, Vicas Publishing House Pvt Ltd., 1977

A notably altered perspective twenty-five years after Everest. Both of these autobiographies required the ghost writer to translate Tenzing's speech into more fluent form. Tenzing's accounts depend entirely on memory. It took months of consultation with others and examination of written materials available in some instances, and extended conversations and interviews with Tenzing, to produce adequately literary and fact-checked books.

8

KURT MANKEN

Kurt Manken and his wife, Nellie, were German Jews who grew up during the first half of the twentieth century in the eastern part of Germany. Kurt's father, according to the story told by my mother, owned a steel mill. Kurt, born around 1890, earned an engineering degree but never worked for a living in Germany. He and Nellie lived on a large estate where their ample mansion opened to deer browsing on wide meadows bordered with thriving forests. His sky-blue eyes and gentle manner bespoke a somewhat tweedy professor. He was thoughtful, intelligent and cultivated.

In 1933 Hitler became Chancellor of Germany. Within five years he had liquidated opposition, moved against Jews in every sphere of German life, consolidated single-party rule, defied the Versailles Treaty, grown the Wehrmacht by ten times to a million men and united Austria and Germany. In November 1938 the Nazis organized Kristallnacht, the Night of the Broken Glass. Pogroms broke out simultaneously all over Germany. Synagogues went up in flames, Jewish shops were looted, homes attacked and many Jews assaulted. In its aftermath, Jews across Germany were subjected to enormous fines to pay for cleaning up the damage. Jewish males were rounded up and sent to concentration camps. In the spring of 1939, Czechoslovakia would fall without a shot fired. Hitler was close to the peak of his popularity and power. Poland's turn would come in the fall. Thereafter the clouds of war would enshroud the organized murder of all but a handful of the European Jews. Even if you could get an immigrant visa, which most could not, 1938 marked essentially the last time Jews had a chance to flee. The Mankens fled. Kurt was in his mid-forties, Nellie a few years younger. They had two school-age children.

They were living in a modest bungalow a few blocks from where my mother, my brother and I lived when, in late 1938, Nellie Manken began coming to the house to give my mother a weekly massage. She kept coming for many years. Little by little—I was a teenager then—I heard highlights of the Manken story.

In late 1938, a recent immigrant, in the middle of middle age, his thinning hair graying, with unemployment at 19% in the "Roosevelt Recession," a diffident man with a heavy German accent, Kurt Manken vainly tried to help support his family by selling Fuller Brushes door-to-door. In those days the Fuller Brush Man was a humbly heroic figure plodding from door to unfriendly door trying to sell brooms, dusters, dustpans, and household sprays. There were very few doorbells that had not been rung by men like these many times before. Those housewives who bought Fuller products already had their regular Fuller Brush Man. Kurt Manken was not likely to become a regular.

A dozen years passed. I had graduated from Caltech. The war was over. I had a good job at the Hughes Aircraft Company. My mother was still getting her weekly massage from Nellie Manken. Kurt remained unemployed. Their children were now teenagers. One day my mother said, "John, you should find a job for Kurt Manken. He is an educated man. He is a graduate engineer. He has never been able to find work. He tried selling Fuller Brushes, but it didn't work. He has sat at home for a dozen years while Nellie supports the family."

I did. My Hughes department included a small drafting room where plans for the Air Force Falcon air-to-air missile were drawn the old-fashioned, pre-computer way: by a room full of draftsmen on high stools leaning over large, translucent vellum sheets at big, sloping drafting tables, each line carefully drawn with a sharp, hard pencil. Every engineer in Kurt's student days, and mine as well, learned how to draft. Kurt, in his late fifties, became a draftsman. I knew he could do it. Delighted, and grateful, he felt useful and wanted. He enjoyed working. He enjoyed meeting people. He felt challenged.

After a few months at Hughes he met Jesse Steinman. Jesse was responsible for analyzing the structural design of the Falcon missile, to be fired by U.S. interceptors at enemy bombers, guided by its own radar to hone in on the target at very high speed. The missile had to withstand tremendous rocket forces at launch and maneuvering accelerations as it twisted and turned on the way to its target.

In those days before digital computers—the early 1950s—the mathematical equations expressing stress in a complex structure could be solved only by arithmetical iteration. You assumed a likely numerical solution to the equations set up in a suitable arithmetical form. Then you used a desktop calculating machine to see if the numbers all fit together. When you discovered that your assumed solution was not quite right, you corrected it slightly and repeated the process. Repeating the process again and again, you eventually find the solution. The missile was constantly being modified. Calculations went on for eight hours every working day, year in and year out.

Jesse needed an assistant who understood the underlying math, to crunch numbers. He offered Kurt the job. Kurt had already been going to night school at UCLA to brush up on the mathematics he had learned some thirty years before. He left the drafting room and, for the next many years he sat in front of a desk-top calculating machine punching keys all day. He invited friends from work to little parties at his home. The small bungalow was furnished with fine furniture from the Mankens' German mansion. A nostalgic oil painting salvaged from the wreckage of their German life portrayed deer grazing on the vast meadow that spread below the rear patio of their long-lost house.

Years passed. Hughes, going through a minor recession, tried to lay him off. He begged them to let him stay. He was over seventy when, in another economic downturn, they finally told him he would have to go.

Some fifteen years after I found a job at Hughes Aircraft for Kurt Manken, my mother had a crippling stroke. It was followed by many others. With each she lost more of her motor and, at last, cognitive functions. Now, more than seven years following the first stroke, she was bedridden, incoherent, attended by nurses around the clock. Dorothy, my wife, having lost a lung to lung cancer the year before, was near the end of her life as multiple metastases slowly worked their way through her bones, her remaining lung and other organs. It was late 1974. The Arab oil embargo of 1973–74 was a daily nightmare. Stocks were falling into the worst bear-market since 1929. After ten years as a corporate vice-president, I was now a business consultant, on my own for the first time in my working life. Times were bad. The future looked worse.

One Sunday morning, the phone rang. It was Nellie Manken. "I haven't heard from Hermine (my mother) in a long time" she said. "How is she?" I told her. Hermine was blind. She could no longer speak. She was paralyzed, and could not turn herself over in bed. She required nurses seven-twenty-four.

Nellie was sorry to hear that. And how was my wife, Dorothy? "Alas," I reported. "She has terminal lung cancer."

"And how is Kurt," I asked.

"Oh," she replied, "I am sorry to say, Kurt died. He died a month ago."

I told her how sorry I was.

"Well," she said, "he caught a virus of some kind. When he didn't improve, they took him to the hospital. He was there only a few days, when he died. He hadn't been sick a day in his life before. I miss him terribly. But it was for the best. He didn't linger. He was eighty-three years old. He had a good life. *Everything worked out for Kurt.*"

Kurt and Nellie had lost their families and many friends to German gas chambers. Kurt lost his fortune, his home, his country and the roots that had nourished more than half his life. His wife had had to change careers in a few weeks from chatelaine to masseuse. He lost his identity and self-worth, idle, unemployed for a dozen years, a stranger in a strange land. They had lived with loss, grieving, fear, anxiety and penury for many of their middle years. But now, at the end of life, adding it all up, Nellie Manken declared: *He had a good life.* Everything worked out for Kurt.

If Hitler had been assassinated after Czechoslovakia but before Poland—April 1939, say—he would have been enshrined as a German hero. He had united the nation with brilliant and chillingly ruthless coups, brilliant oratory, magnificent public spectacles and the politicization and amplification of popular anti-Semitism at home and abroad. His troops had marched unopposed into the Rhineland in 1936, Austria in 1938 and Czechoslovakia in March 1939. Had he been killed after this, before he led Europe to near-universal complicity in the crimes of the Holocaust and the world into the abyss of WWII, his tomb, his monuments, his statues and deeds would have been transmuted into beacons illuminating

German imagination, history and culture for centuries. His statue would gaze sternly from every town square in Germany to this day. But, for Hitler, famously infamous after all, things did not work out well in the end.

My wife, Dorothy, died soon after my conversation with Nellie Manken. A year later I dropped my consulting business and began living by investing. My mother died. Robin and I married. More than a third of a century has passed. We have witnessed fatefully flawed administrations, tragic and still unresolved wars, a potentially catastrophic economic and credit crisis, tectonic shifts of production and wealth, the global menace of melting ice and of rising seas, growing world population, mounting pollution, and the world-wide clash of mutually alien civilizations. Millions suffer a harsh, bitter present to which all their yesterdays have led. Just about everyone labors under shadowing burdens of feared futures.

Aristotle tells us that you cannot decide whether a man has had a "happy" life—a life of fulfillment and flourishing lived according to virtue—until he dies. Thirty-five some years ago my circumstances and prospects, though incomparably better than Kurt's at the nadir of his life, did not look or feel good. But as these reflections are brought to an end, the writer, at eighty-nine, is still in good health, with ample vigor. Robin, younger, is, too. Our marriage is happy. It seems, with the end not so far off, I, too, have had a good life, an outcome I would have thought barely possible in 1974. Like Kurt, everything has worked out for me—for us—too.

So far, that is.

So far.

NOTES

CHAPTER 5—CURTIS LeMAY

1. Minuteman's design flaws were eventually corrected. Two years of stonewalling passed before any Air Force action was taken. Ultimately, about 1,000 missiles were activated.

CHAPTER 6—THE SKYBOLT CRISIS

1. Indeed, Skybolt was discussed at a British Cabinet meeting two weeks after initial funding for Skybolt was released by the DoD. The costs of continuing the British Blue Streak ballistic missile project were compared with acquiring Skybolt missiles and with acquiring Polaris submarines, all this nearly a month *before* Macmillan met with Eisenhower to close a deal on Skybolt! I am deeply indebted to Ron Landa of the Historical Office of the Office of the Secretary of Defense for sending me, along with several other documents only fairly recently available, *Note of a Meeting at 10 Downing Street, 20 February, 1960,* attended by the Prime minister, Minister of Aviation, Minister of Defence, and others. *CAB 131/23: Cabinet Defence Committee Minutes and Papers, The National Archives,* (hereafter abbreviated as TNA)
2. It is probable that Secretary Gates, his deputy, James Douglas, and the Assistant Secretary for International Security affairs, Jack Irwin, secured copies at or soon after the Camp David meeting. All were replaced by the incoming Kennedy Administration in January 1961. Neither McNamara nor, apparently, anyone else on the American team at the Nassau Conference, had a copy until I secured one as described near the end of this account.
3. Gates was sworn in as SecDef on December 2, 1959. He had been Secretary of the Navy. Skybolt was started by the Air Force in early 1959, and the British-American collaboration that gave birth to it began months before in 1958. It

is quite unlikely that Gates knew anything about Skybolt until briefed prior to the Camp David meeting.

4. The Zuckerman archives are housed at the University of East Anglia, Norwich, in 1250 boxes occupying 650 linear feet. They include a formidable collection of papers, documents and books ranging from anatomical studies, animal behavior, population, family planning, WWII bombing studies, and the NATO Science Committee and the Pugwash Movement, to name only a few.

5. Quinlan, Michael, "Cabinets and the Bomb" Workshop, (Session Two), *The British Academy Review*, March 27, 2007.
www.britac.ac.uk/pubs/review/perspectives/0703cabinetsandbomb-2.html.

6. Zuckerman (1988), 253

7. Ibid, 237 et seq.

8. Ibid, 239.

9. Lavery, Brian, "The British government and the American Polaris base in the Clyde," *Journal for Maritime Research,* September 2001,
www.jmr.nmm.ac.uk/server?show=/conJmrArticle.2&set

10. For a fully referenced summary, see Landa, 123

11. Landa, 126.

12. Ibid, 126.

13. In the fall 1962, when the British were deeply concerned that Skybolt might be cancelled, the British Air Attaché in Washington sent a message to a number of British officials analyzing the key factors in play on the U.S. side, stating "The acrimony already generated between McNamara and LeMay over the R.S. 70 could well develop into a public row of even greater dimension which might at least prevent hasty decisions being taken and give us room to maneuver." Memo, Air Vice-Marshal R.H.E. Emson (Air Attaché, Washington) for Chief of Air Staff Marshal Thomas G. Pike, November 2, 1962, Air 19/1076, Air Ministry: Private Office Papers, TNA. The decisions were anything but hasty, and the potential for such a row had been envisioned long before. British officers in the U.S. reporting to the Ministries in London did not read the demise of the B-70 correctly.

14. Neustadt (1999), 27-28

15. Ibid, 30.

16. Ibid, 31.

17. Ibid, 31.

18. Ibid, 32-3. The news reaching Thorneycroft, chiefly from British officers stationed in the U.S., fluctuated widely. On October 31, 1962, Group Capt. Fryer signaled that an important Project Change Proposal for Skybolt had been approved by McNamara on August 31. By October 31 he was threatening

to cancel Skybolt unless its November 8 flight test "were an unqualified success. . . this reversal of form indicates plainly to me that McNamara is still being subjected to pressure from those elements within his own organization that are unenthusiastic about SKYBOLT." He concluded that all was not lost. Production funds were being released, "and perhaps of greater significance than any other factor the RS-70 is as good as dead." (Fryer for Cornford et al, October 31, 1962, DEFE 13/409, Ministry of Defence Private Offices: Registered Files, TNA) Like others, this message was long on political conspiracy implications and short on meaningful technical assessments.

19. Ibid, 31-3.
20. Ibid, 38.
21. Ibid, 41.
22. I have summarized most of the foregoing chronology of November-December events from Neustadt, 36-69. Neustadt's study was prepared for President Kennedy in 1963. It remained classified for 29 years, and was not published until 1999. Numerous British documents withheld from Neustadt, classified for decades, have been declassified and made available to scholars since then. See also Kaplan, Landa & Drea (2005), 375-84.
23. Neustadt, op.cit., 70.
24. Zuckerman, op. cit., 251. Solly cites notes I had taken at the meeting.
25. Neustadt, op. cit.,71-4. All the following citations in Neustadt were taken from a copy of my notes.
26. Zuckerman, op. cit., 239.
27. Ibid, 251-52.
28. Report, Air Marshall C. H. Hartley, "The Nassau Talks," undated, T 325/88, Treasury: R.W.B. Clarke Papers, TNA. This was a lawyer's *plaidoyer*. Thorneycroft had cancelled Blue Streak for many reasons overlapping the American rationale for cancelling Skybolt. He states that Dr. Carl Covington, a junior member of my Pentagon office, was one of his back-grounding informants. I have no recollection whatever that Covington had any involvement with the Skybolt project. Ron Landa has told me, however, that Covington was occasionally in touch with British officials who were seeking information about it. They should have come to me.
29. Ibid, 5. See also a report by another of the British technical advisers, James Lighthill of the Ministry of Aviation, who concluded that I really knew very little about missile and guidance technology. (Lighthill, "The Bahamas Conference: Report on Attendance as Part of the Ministry of Defence Party," undated. AVIA 65/1851, Ministry of Supply and successor Departments: Registered Files, TNA.) If my talks with him were not my finest hour, it

remains that I was a senior member of the Hughes team that designed, built and successfully demonstrated (1950) the first airborne celestial-inertial navigation system in the world.

30. Zuckerman, op. cit., 254

31. In his memo of November 2 (see footnote 13), Air Vice-Marshall Emson concluded: "The damage which Sir Solly [Zuckerman] has done to our interests has certainly been sufficient to lead the anti-Skybolt lobby to believe that we should not oppose too strongly a decision [by the Americans] to cancel. In the last few months we have done our best to retrieve the situation by representations at all levels, culminating in the recent Thorneycroft visit, and if we can have an unequivocal letter from Sir Solly it may finally convince Ruebel (sic) and Brown [the DDR&E] that we mean business." It appears that British interests (i.e.: those for "don't cancel Skybolt no matter what") had been damaged by Solly urging a supposed "anti-Skybolt lobby" to lie low. Emson apparently felt that the damage just *might* be repaired if Solly would compose a letter of contrition that would, in turn, influence Harold Brown and me.

CHAPTER 7—TENSING NORGAY

1. A description of this expedition by the Royal Geographic Society (Great Britain) lists the name of every British climber, but not Tenzing's.

2. A "col" is a pass between two mountain peaks (Old Fr., neck). The South Col lies between Mt. Everest and Lhotsé, the first and fourth highest mountains in the world. The South Col is usually swept by high winds, leaving it fairly free of snow. Here climbers have entered the "death zone" above 8,000 meters. Altitude sickness is a substantial threat. It is hard to sleep. Most climbers can digest food slowly or not at all. One cannot survive here or higher for more than 2-3 days. Forced too long into tents at the col by bad weather, climbers must turn back, and rarely get a second chance to return unless on a future expedition.

3. In 1938 20 rupees were worth about $7.40, nominally equivalent to about $100 in 2009.

4. They were only 800 feet below the summit. See endnote 2, above, re: the "death zone."

5. Sherpas are ethnic Tibetans whose ancestors lived at altitudes up to 14,000 feet for 25,000 years. Tests have shown that on average they require much lower caloric intake than Caucasians at high altitudes, and are notably less

susceptible to weight loss and other high-altitude illnesses.

6. Bourdillon worked with his physician father to design a closed-circuit oxygen system, but it has not come into wide use. His colleagues agreed that had he and Evans struggled to the top, they probably would have perished. Three years later Bourdillon, 31, fell to his death while rock-climbing. He had been a rocket designer. Evans was a brain surgeon.

7. Actually, he ran off to Kathmandu when he was only thirteen. Brought back by his family, who sent him to a monastery to be brought up as a monk, he ran away again. Back home for several years, he fled at nineteen to Darjeeling with some young companions. There, after a couple of years as a farmhand, he was finally able to begin his mountaineering career, starting as a "coolie."

8. He writes, however, that "... my present name was given me on the insistence of a lama who had found from the holy books that I was the reincarnation of a rich man of Solu Khumbu who had recently died. Tenzing Norgay was not that rich man's name, but the lama thought that a name that meant 'wealthy-fortunate follower of religion' would be best for one for whom he predicted great things."

CPSIA information can be obtained at www.ICGtesting.com
Printed in the USA
LVOW06s2054131013

356693LV00001B/63/P